LESSONS FROM COVID 19

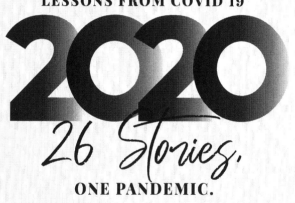

2020

26 Stories,

ONE PANDEMIC.

Dedicated to those who
survived 2020

ISBN: 978-1-7353610-4-8

Unless otherwise expressed, all quotations and references must be permitted by Authors. All scripture references from NKJ and NIV Bibles.

Cover Design:

Business Startup & Marketing Solutions LLC and JWG Publishing House.

Published by

JWG Publishing

Printed in the United States of America.

TABLE OF CONTENTS

FROM THE VISIONARY:
Joan Wright-Good   VIII

INTRODUCTION:
The Breath of God 2020
Tameka Echols   VI

CHAPTER ONE:
Discovering Self-Awareness during the 2020
COVID-19 Pandemic
Robert H. Marshall, Jr.   1

CHAPTER TWO:
The Year of the Game Changer
Genevieve Carvil-Harris   7

CHAPTER THREE:
Essential Encouragement
Carlene C. Wright   13

CHAPTER FOUR:
That's What Friends Are For
Cherolyn Davis   22

CHAPTER FIVE:
Companionship in the Middle of a Pandemic
and in the Midst of a Crisis
Aldith Lowe   29

CHAPTER SIX:
Grieve Yourself Back to Life
Keesha Barreau   39

CHAPTER SEVEN:
Healing Lessons from COVID-19
James Steward   48

CHAPTER EIGHT:
His Grace Is Sufficient for Me—

God Can Bless You in Any Season!

Diana Sharpe   55

CHAPTER NINE:

Unprecedented Times Call for
Unprecedented Partnerships

Shedly Casseus-Parnther   66

PART 2   72

CHAPTER TEN:

Fear Is Not Your Portion

Marva Bozeman   73

CHAPTER ELEVEN:

They Say That 2020 Is Perfect Vision; Is It?

Petula Barclay   81

CHAPTER TWELVE:

Can We Breathe?

Sharon Patterson-Capek   89

CHAPTER THIRTEEN:

Reflections, Divine Purpose

Megan and Prince Aderele   94

CHAPTER FOURTEEN:

Called to Serve Despite Adversity

Nicole Small-Fletcher   103

CHAPTER FIFTEEN:

2020 the Year of Humbling

Grace Ann Long   108

CHAPTER SIXTEEN:

Heaven's P.P.P. (Preparation for Progress
in a Pandemic)

LaWanda C. Harris   112

CHAPTER SEVENTEEN:

I Was Not Ready for the Final Chapter
Que Johnson   121

PART 3   125

CHAPTER EIGHTEEN:
The Genesis
Dr. Punitha Rathnam   126
CHAPTER NINETEEN:
COVID Chronicles
Sonia White   129
CHAPTER TWENTY:
Vision 2020—What Do You See?
Mya Smith-Edmonds   138
CHAPTER TWENTY-ONE:
Testing the Depth of Stacey Lynn
Stacey Emerson   149
CHAPTER TWENTY-TWO:
The Sunshine in the Dark
Sunita White   155
CHAPTER TWENTY-THREE:
What's in Your 'Fridge? (A Cry for Help)
Sharon Betts   162
CHAPTER TWENTY-FOUR:
Surviving the Most Frightening 2020 Moment
Rosetta Hutchinson   169
CHAPTER TWENTY-FIVE:
Let's Sum This All Up!
Dei Tatum   178

FROM THE VISIONARY

DR. JOAN WRIGHT GOOD

Hey there, Change Agent, welcome to history set in the year 2020. If you've never heard of me before, where have you been? It's about time we meet. My name is Joan Wright-Good, and I am a Cycle Breaker and History Maker. As a first-generation Strategic business service CEO and self-taught (but God-ordained) Publisher I have helped thousands of entrepreneurs, executives, brands, and authors to become unstuck and overcome their personal insecurities, passion thieves, limiting beliefs, brand invisibility, and financial challenges. I lead this charge by example, using the concepts I teach to create multiple seven figures.

Today, you are about to witness some of the lives that were impacted by my gift, and I know you will subsequently be impacted by their lives as well. It's no secret that 2020 was a unique year so when God gave me the idea to have a group of people, from different persuasions, countries, and cultures contribute to a global historical artifact, I had no precocity that this would have been the result. I knew it would be a source of history for decades to come but I had no idea that within the pages healing would lurk.

The book *Lessons from Covid 19, 2020 - 26 stories one pandemic* is one of the leading descriptive source and language, of 2020. The book will be ubiquitous in the publishing industry, in resource interchange, and the global transformation pace. This is partly due to the dynamic diversity of the authors and their stories.

Who Should Read This Book?

We've tried to write a book that serves as a generational posterity, with some optional subject matter interludes, giving you the chance to take away as much as your reading pallet can take. *Lessons from Covid 19, 2020 - 26 stories one pandemic* is suitable for everyone.

Enjoy!

INTRODUCTION:

THE BREATH OF GOD 2020

TAMEKA ECHOLS

In early March 2020, and seemingly out of nowhere, news stations around the world began broadcasting about a virus that was causing people illness, overwhelming suffering, and even death. A few people had mild symptoms, but countless others experienced profoundly serious conditions. Reports of coughing, fever, fatigue, sore throat, and, in some cases, difficulty breathing were common among all who had succumbed to the bug. Many people unwittingly infected others because it could take up to fourteen days before people showed symptoms. As the virus reproduced and progressed throughout the population, reports emerged that its origin was Wuhan, China, and it was spreading like a wildfire from country to country. While specialists attempted to determine, albeit unsuccessfully, how the virus came to be, they could confirm that it could be transmitted through the respiratory system. Transmission from person to person occurs through droplets expelled from the nose or mouth.

The World Health Organization (WHO) named this new strain of coronavirus COVID-19, and the virus is now responsible for causing a global pandemic. According to the *New York Times* database, as of November 4, 2020, "more than 9,468,700 people in the United States have been infected with the coronavirus and at least 232,600 have died." The Center for Systems Science and Engineering John Hopkins University reports as of November 4, 2020, 47,675,228 people were infected by this virus, and 1,217,745 people have died globally.

On the evening of March 19, 2020, I began to feel heavy pressure on my chest and felt like I could not breathe. I was anxious, panic was creeping up on me, and I did not know what to do. Fear was trying to overwhelm me. So, I began to pray and cry out to God asking, "Lord, what is this?" and, "Jesus, help me!" He shared with me that this is the feeling that so many others are experiencing right now and will continue to feel in times to come. They will need prayer, intercessory prayer, from a heart posture of compassion.

The Lord said that we have the "pneuma," the very breath of God that resides within us that regulates our lungs, heart, brain, and respiratory system; so, we have nothing to fear! The Lord spoke to my spirit, saying:

> Breathe out stress and breathe in peace.
> Breathe out worry and breathe in trust.
> Breathe out fear and breathe in His presence.
> Breathe out doubt and breathe in confidence.
> Breathe out anxiety and breathe in calmness.
> Breathe out despair and breathe in God's light.
> Breathe out anger and breathe in forgiveness.
> Breathe out bitterness and breathe in kindness.
> Breathe out impatience and breathe in patience.
> Breathe out depression and breathe in cheerfulness.
> Breathe out death and breathe in life.
> Breathe out weakness and breathe in strength.
> Breathe out timidity and breathe in courage.
> Breathe out pain and breathe in wellness.
> Breathe out sadness and breathe in gladness.
> Breathe out discouragement and breathe in hope.
> Breathe out hate and breathe in love.
> Breathe out unhappiness and breathe in joy.

Breathe out sickness and breathe in healing.

I spoke all of these words from my mouth, and immediately the heaviness, the pressure, and the difficulty with breathing left me. The anxiety, fear, and panic I had disappeared and has not returned! I am at peace! To God be the glory!

God, the Lord, created the heavens and stretched them out. He created the earth and everything in it. He gives breath to everyone and life to everyone who walks the earth (Isaiah 42:5).

Take time to praise the Lord for every breath that He has given. Every breath that we take is the gift of life and should not be taken for granted.

PART I

CHAPTER ONE:

DISCOVERING SELF-AWARENESS DURING THE 2020 COVID-19 PANDEMIC

ROBERT H. MARSHALL, JR.

I remember it so clearly. It was a normal day in the office when I received a not-so-normal call from my wife around two in the afternoon informing me about the city shut down that was about to happen over the next couple of months because of the rising numbers of COVID-19 cases. I will never forget hearing the panic in her tone and inflections. As a husband, I was more concerned with her well-being than I was the actual pandemic.

The first words that I blurted out were, "What do you need me to do?"

As a good wife and mother would do, she said, "Pick up the kids."

I left work three hours early, but before picking up my three toddlers, I went by my favorite store that always had what I needed, Walgreens (the one that's "located on the corner of happy and healthy"). Upon my arrival, I had already made a mental list of the items I needed to ensure we would be OK during this pandemic. I went through every aisle, picking everything that I thought I needed, like napkins, coloring books, vitamins, Tylenol, food, and cases of water. As soon as I approached the home cleaning supply isles, I saw they were already out of toilet paper, disinfectant spray, wipes, and sanitizer. I had no idea this would be a snapshot of the rest of 2020, a year filled with surprises, uncertainty, fear, new norms, and self-discovery.

My name is Robert Marshall, and prior to the pandemic I took an unhealthy pride in my accomplishments as a working middle-class, semi-successful husband, father, educator, mentor, counselor, and whatever other titles and positions I held that I thought made me a "good man."

That was just it. I was able to exude my prominence, prestige, and accomplishments as badges of honor to prove to the world that I was somebody and deserved to be recognized, loved, and respected.

Little did I know that this pandemic shutdown would awaken all of the internal voices that I could previously drown out with the busyness and demands of my career, business, and life. COVID put a stop to all of it. My badges of success started to collect dust, and my need for attention and affirmation started to implode. I started to crumble. The goal-oriented, successful man was left to contend with the giant wounds from his adolescence. The silence forced me to see and hear the cries of the inner boy whose father acted like he never existed. He felt every touch from the wolves dressed in clergy who ripped apart his innocence and self-worth in the name of Jesus. I had to face the fact that for the majority of my adult life I wore my accomplishments like caked-on makeup in hopes that no one would see the broken, fragile boy pretending to be a man.

Who would have thought that a national health pandemic would force me to deal with me? As I processed with close friends, I concluded that I was not the only person running away from the pain from the past. One of my best friends shared that he realized he had never forgiven his mother for abandoning him and his brothers to live her dream life with her boyfriend in another country. One of my other friends told me he was not able to sleep at night because he kept having flashbacks of him and his mother as they were repeatedly assaulted by his father. He told me that in every dream he kept hearing and seeing his father whip him while saying, "I'm going to make a man out of you."

Though from quite different lives and cultural backgrounds, we all were being whipped by our pasts, one that forced us into unhealthy understandings of what it means to be a man. After much dialogue, we came together and created a list of five principles that would put us on a journey to healing. We knew that we were not to blame for our trauma, but our healing was our personal responsibility. We gave each other permission to redefine our understanding of what it means to be a man. The truth is we spent countless years trying to define our "maleness" and, in the process, made a whole lot of mistakes while encountering even more growing pains. We were done with the toxic definitions that we were taught and the ones that we caught from other unhealthy men. We gave our selves a rite of passage and realized that a boy finds manhood not through cultural expectation but through inner values. He does not live by external pressures but by internal principles. We realized that even though we were all born into horrific situations, we could choose to be whole men.

Secondly, we realized that no matter what happened to us, it didn't have to define us. We made declarations that we were worthy of all the divine chose to bestow upon us. Realizing that, we saw our own thoughts of inadequacy housed in our minds and emotions, not only trespassing but also lying to us for years, never allowing us to fully embrace our true identity. It was like drinking a slow-drip poison; we didn't feel the effects until it was too late. Our morning declarations gave us the courage to evict the lies of inadequacy and inferiority.

Lastly, we all realized that we had a responsibility to share these newfound revelations with other men contending with their own traumas. This was truly a matter of faith over fear. Out of this, we launched our benefit corporation I Am Man, Inc., which seeks to empower men to become the best versions of themselves. We also launched a podcast to amplify and raise awareness of the various lived experiences of every man regardless of his pedigree.

The 2020 pandemic gave us the time and space to think big but dream bigger. We were given permission to dream again, to feel again, and to live beyond the expectations of our personal and financial limitations. We were able to throw away our shiny badges of success that we once wore with honor. We finally found our space in the world! This was our purpose that gave us the power to re-write our own narratives and gave us the ability to help other men rewrite theirs.

Dr. Tony Evans frequently says, "If you want a better world, develop stronger countries, and if you want stronger countries, then develop stronger states, and if you want stronger states, then develop stronger cities, and if you want stronger cities, then develop stronger neighborhoods, and if you want stronger neighborhoods, then develop stronger families and if you want stronger families, we must strengthen men." Charles Dickens sums up the COVID pandemic nicely: "It was the best of times, it was the worst of times, it was the epoch of belief, it was the epoch of incredulity, it was he season of light, it was the season of darkness, it was the spring of hope, it was also the winter of despair."

CHAPTER TWO:

THE YEAR OF THE GAME CHANGER

GENEVIEVE CARVIL-HARRIS

Success is to be measured not so much by the position that one has reached in life as by the obstacles which he has overcome.—Booker T. Washington

Success can only be defined by the individual on life's journey. However, success is to be measured by the obstacles someone has to overcome to reach it. When I sat down in 2019 to make plans for my new year, I did so from an optimistic and inspiring place. The year was set to be one of the best that I had ever witnessed: 2020. It was to be a year of clarity, of purpose, and of strategic design. I have always been a planner who expects great things from what is presented to me, but I was not prepared for the year that will forever be remembered as 2020.

I was prepared for transition; I had told my supervisor in December that I would be leaving my job to pursue full-time entrepreneurship. I had been working faithfully in my job in education from when I got married in 2014. This decision was not an easy one, but I had reached the point of my greatest capacity within the company, and it was time to spread my wings by returning to entrepreneurship. The original plan was for me to leave during spring break, but my supervisor asked me to graduate with my students so that they would not be sad or distracted for the rest of the year. I agreed, but once spring break came, we received the news that the country was going to be shut down. COVID-19 had shifted everyone's plans, including my own, and now we would have to slow our lives down and remain quarantined until further notice. I was in middle school when 9/11 occurred, and the memories are still fresh in my mind. This pandemic has had a greater impact because the entire world has been affected.

I saw individuals lose their jobs and families be torn apart by social distancing while being sick. Throughout the course of this pandemic, I personally lost twenty people from as young as twenty years old to elders, and it truly took a toll on my emotions and my mind. Funerals during the pandemic were almost as heart-wrenching as the news of the death. Most of the individuals had to die alone as family members were not allowed to be in the rooms with them, even if the cause of death weren't COVID-19 related. The effect of the pandemic was widespread. I would have been depressed if not for knowing my purpose and having a strategy for my life. One of the greatest memories that I have from this time came out of one of the darkest moments of the year. I received news that one of my close friends had died, and I immediately felt low and heartbroken, but instead of falling into a depressed state, I made a commitment to help over 200 aspiring entrepreneurs build a brand and establish methods of financial stability. I refer to them as "game changers" because they have learned to use their skill sets to change the game of their lives and set up wealth that can be passed down for generations. I have been able to help them achieve their first five, six, and even seven figure months and that has been the joy of my year. This year has been a rough one, to say the least; however, I have been able to overcome difficulties and become successful because I have learned the following lessons, and I hope you will too.

1. **Identify the void in your life and what you need to fill it.**

   There are many areas in your life that may feel empty because of the absence of a desired outcome in life. Some people can have dream jobs that lack purpose and fulfillment and leave them feeling hopeless, miserable, and stuck. I had to identify the voids that my life decisions had created and the tools that I needed to study to fill them. I discovered that most of the issues that I encountered came from a lack of resources, and when I became more resourceful and researched the areas that I was weak in, I was able to feel more confident and approach life better.

2. **Discover your skillset, and make it profitable.**

   It's crucial to remind yourself of who you are and what you were born to do. It's a common saying that the second most important day of someone's life is when they discover the reason they were born. You can figure this out by accurately assessing what skillset you are naturally drawn to. I was drawn to business and money-generating activities from childhood, and it was best for me to come back to entrepreneurship to fulfill my purpose. This journey led me to make intentional efforts to monetize my skill sets, and I was able to discover ways to make the things that I loved profitable.

3. **Do not disregard your sense of value.**

   One of my toughest lessons for me was that I taught people how to treat me. This meant that I had a role in the way that people valued me. I experienced a lack of appreciation from others because I never stood up for myself or my value. This is an important lesson because if you do not know your value, others will convince you that you deserve less. You must study your market to ensure that you are honoring the value that you bring to others.

4. **Give yourself the freedom to dream without judgment.**
One of the biggest mistakes that I see people make when approaching the realization of their dreams is comparing their previous successes and winning moments to the ones they are currently pursuing. Many fall into a trap here because they do not forgive themselves for their role in failed endeavors and initiatives. If you do not dream without judgment, you will find yourself stagnant and full of questions.

5. **Embrace the idea that you are worthy of the wealth that you will receive.**
The crown jewel in allowing yourself to become a game changer is found in this step. After identifying your value, one of the biggest pieces in the journey to success is knowing that you are worthy of the wealth that comes with it. Riches are not wealth, although they can include them. If you find yourself struggling in this area, remember that wealth also speaks to an abundance of valuable possessions, and your relationships are definitely included. I tell my clients all the time that relationships are the new form and longer-lasting

version of currency. I'm here to encourage you, so that when you realize that it is time to achieve your highest level of success, you must shift your mindset to embrace the true wealth of life that you will be receiving.

CHAPTER THREE

ESSENTIAL ENCOURAGEMENT

CARLENE C. WRIGHT

Let's take a moment to journey back to December 31, 2019, 11:59 p.m. Where were you? What were you doing? Let's take it a step further, what were some of your goals, dreams, or anticipations about entering a new decade?

If you are like most of us, you made your "boss" plans

and were excited and ready to take 2020 by storm. I sure made my plans. I had entrepreneurial goals to restructure both of my businesses, Wright Encouragement and Wright Insurance Firm. I made personal plans to equip myself with the word of God so that I can teach others, become a published author, and to pay off a substantial amount of debt to name a few.

On January 24, 2020, Wright Encouragement, LLC hosted an event called "Vision Up 2020" - A Vision Planning and Networking Experience. The room was filled with approximately 80 participants ready to "plan, prepare, and pray," as was our theme. We worked through a vibrant agenda with great speakers, sponsors, prizes, food, and fun. We wrote the vision that we felt God placed in our hearts and portrayed it on our vision boards. It was an electrifying experience as we left the event with lots of hope and readiness to execute and win! Subsequently, two months later, COVID -19 became a global pandemic that changed our lives from what we called "normal" and pushed us into a "new normal."

It is now ten months later, December 2020, and it is as if the world has been turned upside down. It is reported that over 80,000,000 people have been affected by COVID -19 with fatalities of over 1,700,000. The loss of these lives was untimely and devastating. We have lost fathers, mothers, sisters, brothers, and friends. Their homes will never be the same as we memorialize them as "loved ones - gone too soon."

The government ordered mandatory shutdowns; some small businesses closed their doors; many individuals lost their jobs; most churches transitioned their services to online; people were quarantined at home; schools transitioned from the classroom to home schooling; and some professionals were identified as essential workers. The word *"essential"* came to the forefront and gained a new appreciation. Needless to say, many people were gravely disturbed by the things were happening and disappointed as to how the year 2020 unfolded. These were unprecedented times; we have never seen anything like this before.

These unprecedented times and new normal called for a higher level of individual strength. It called for each person to find one thing that would sustain their spirits and evoke their souls to connect with hope, one thing that would ground them and redirect them to keep moving forward, one thing that would raise up a giant on the inside to relinquish fear and hold on to vision and possibilities. This one thing was without a doubt essential. This one thing is encouragement; *"Essential Encouragement"* from the word of God.

The word essential denotes that something is absolutely necessary and extremely important. Encouragement is the act of giving support, confidence, or hope. When God placed the desire in my heart to start Wright Encouragement a few years ago, it was with the intent to support others in their everyday life journey. I wanted to encourage them to believe that with faith in God, hope, and love they can make it through the rough times. 2020 is considered to be one of those rough times.

As believers, we were tested to evaluate what our faith in God truly meant and how we were applying its practicality in our everyday lives. This evaluation evoked questions such as, "Are you placing your faith in the economy, people, your abilities, or in God's sovereignty?" In effect, it placed a mirror in front of each person and demanded answers that would set the pace for how their faith would stand in the face of these obstacles in these unprecedented times.

For many, their notion of faith demonstrated that no matter what took place with the occurrences of the global pandemic or anything else that happened this year, their trust in God's sovereignty would stand. There is a scripture that I hold dear and it says, "You will keep in perfect peace those whose minds are steadfast because they trust in you." (Isaiah 26:23). On March 22, 2020, I participated in a panel interview at the Faith Center Ministries in Sunrise, FL hosted by renowned leader, Bishop Henry Fernandez. Bishop Fernandez is a proponent for encouraging people to have faith in God.

Throughout the pandemic he has been intentional with making the effort to 10X the encouragement that he gives through inspiring messages, podcast, blog post, text messages, and Facebook lives. In essence, the purpose of the interview was to encourage the viewers to stay connected to the word of God during the pandemic. I used the above Bible verse as an essential scripture to encourage over 3,000 viewers. I knew that the uncertainties that surrounded us would be accompanied by an attack of fear, anxiety, and situational depression. To fight this kind of attack, we were going to have to lean into the weight and security of this and other scriptures to stay encouraged.

The events of this year reaffirmed that whatever it is that we are up against in life, there is a scripture in the Bible that will encourage us and give us strength and hope to make it through. If you are dealing with an illness, divorce, grief, financial downfall, family dilemma, career crisis, depression, anxiety, or hopelessness there is a scripture with your name on it. God loves us so much that he left us with recourse from the scriptures to get through the rough times. Here are some others scriptures that are essential in keeping us encouraged, especially during a pandemic.

Essential Encouragement Scriptures

- For God has not given us a spirit of fear, but of power and of love and of a sound mind (2 Timothy 1:7).

- Be still and know that I am God (Psalms 37:10).

- For I know the plans I have for you, declares the Lord, plans to prosper you and not to harm you, plans to give you hope and a future (Jeremiah 29:11).

- Now unto Him that is able to do exceedingly abundantly above all that we ask or think, according to the power that worketh in us (Ephesians 3:20).

- The steadfast love of the Lord never ceases; his mercies never come to an end; they are new every morning; great is your faithfulness (Lamentations 3:22-23).

These scriptures were essential to get us through the rough times in 2020. They encouraged us to keep our hope up and to have faith in God. It is a good practice to commit some of these scriptures to memory. When they are committed to memory, you can easily say them out loud or meditate on them as my mother often encourages. Each week, I wrote a new scripture on an index card and taped it on my bathroom mirror so that it would be in plain sight every morning. I used this simple method to memorize several scriptures. Before we continue, I have a question for you. As you read the list above, which one of these scriptures stood out for you? Which one of them do you need to commit to memory? I want to challenge you to select one and memorize it. Here is an exercise that can help you memorize scriptures.

Scripture Memorization Execution (SME)

1. Select a scripture - Look at the list of scriptures above and pick one that you would like to memorize.

2. Make a visual - Write it on an index card, piece of paper, or type it on the notepad in your phone and make it your screen saver.

3. Execute - Read the scripture for seven consecutive days until you have memorized it.

One day, the scriptures you have memorized will be needed to keep you encouraged or to encourage someone else. For example, as I mentioned earlier, one of the goals that I set out to accomplish this year, was to pay off a substantial amount of debt. The finances to accomplish this goal would come from the restructuring of my businesses. Like for most people, the nature of the pandemic hindered my ability to see clients in person as I normally would; which initially caused a financial impact. I started to think about future dating this goal for 2021 and resetting my expectations toward it. My mind raced with thoughts like, I am a single woman so I need to pinch every penny and save what I can this year and not worry about paying off any debt because what if, and what if, ect. and ect.

The Holy Spirit brought this scripture back to my memory to encourage me, "Be still, and know that I am God" (Psalms 37:10). The scripture reminded me not to make hasty decisions that God had not sanctioned. It quickly snatched me from opening my mind to accepting thoughts of lack instead of operating in the abundance mindset that God has given me. Sometimes we allow what we see and feel to change our mind away from what we are striving to accomplish. We change our minds from believing what God has promised to believe what we are predicting. We are encouraged to have faith when we do not see the evidence. If we can see the evidence of something, then there is no need for faith (Hebrews 11:1).

Our big God is not confined by our little plans or a global pandemic. He is the "I AM that I AM" (Exodus 3:14), and I needed to be still. After this moment, I pivoted to implementing new strategies for both Wright Encouragement and Wright Insurance Firm. God made a way for me to pay off over $26,000 in debt during this pandemic while still supporting my local church and giving to others in need. I was thankful and ecstatic about that, and then He took it a step further. He provided the perfect situation for me to refinance my home with no administrative fees, a lower interest rate, and lower payments. Additionally, the strategic business changes have now shaped the restructuring of my businesses. (#GodDidIt.) God did exceedingly, abundantly far above what I could ask or think according to His power that worked in me. (Ephesian 3:20).

I shared this story and the lessons that it taught me to encourage you to keep the essential word of God in our mind and heart. You cannot afford to miss out on what God is saying and doing; even in the rough times. God speaks to us through His words, not ours. Furthermore, the Bible tells us that the Holy Spirit will bring the word of God back to our remembrance; our job is to make sure that it is there in the first place (St. John 14:26). Had I not been encouraged by that scripture during the pandemic; this story would have had a different ending. If you have a goal or dream that you want to postpone for a later date because of circumstances not in your favor, allow God to speak to you before you reset it. Do not miss your moment! Your story may be different from mine; however, we share the same opportunity for a good ending. When you embrace encouragement through the word of God it changes your perspective, creates a new narrative, and gives you a better story for his glory.

As we look back on the year 2020, we can do so with gratitude realizing that regardless of what took place with the global pandemic, we made it through! We are still here to live out God's plan for our lives. We do not know what 2021 or the years to come will bring, but we can rest assure that the essential word of God will give us the *right encouragement* to believe bigger and to hold on to this truth, "the steadfast love of the Lord never ceases; His mercies never come to an end; they are new every morning; great is His faithfulness!"

CHAPTER FOUR:
THAT'S WHAT FRIENDS ARE FOR

CHEROLYN DAVIS

Knowing you can always count on me, for sure/That's what friends are for/For good times and bad times/I'll be on your side forevermore.-That's what friends are for
—Dionne Warwick

Imagine being eight years old moving into a new neighborhood, having to attend a new school, and trying to understand why it all had to happen. After we pulled into our new driveway to our new three-bedrooms, two-bath home, my stepdad put the car in park, and I begin to exit our yellow Volkswagen with my white Barbie tucked firmly under my arm. As I walked to the front door and glanced across the street, there stood the Walker sisters waving as if to say hi. I stood there wondering if I should wave back; ten seconds later I performed the same wave, which opened up a newly found friendship of sleepovers, carpools, tea parties, deep secrets, and boyfriend stories that lasted for over four decades.

Fast-forward to the year 2020, a year no one could have ever imagine or think of a year in which more than 296,000 Americans passed away due to this thing called COVID-19, The Corona Virus, or The Pandemic of 2020, which caused us to become uncomfortable, depressed, scared, and filled with anxiety. Our hope for 2020 was for our vision that we had written down and made plain to elevate, expand, and enlarge our territories and connections, to no avail. Those visions were blurred and blinded. This season during the pandemic has also dislocated families and caused friendships to shut down, crumble, and expose cracks in the best-friend relationships that may have been there all along.

As if things weren't already trying, a childhood friend of mine and I were discussing life and where we saw ourselves in the next two to three years. We are reaching fifty years of age, and we haven't accomplished much or completed the goals we've set for ourselves. Now, I thought that was a fair question to ask her as I asked myself the same question. Apparently, I offended her with my question, and this is where the destruction of our friendship during the pandemic began. Never did I think I would have offended her. I mean, we were like Mike Lawry and Marcus Burnett from *Bad Boys* or perhaps even the leads in *Thelma & Louise*. We talked daily, had family trips, enjoyed family outings and social activities, and clubbed and partied. We did everything together. April and I were friends for over twenty-plus years; her children call me Auntie, and my children do the same with her, so why wouldn't we do everything together?

After the conversation with April, I begin to reflect on my life, my career, and spiritual growth, reevaluating who I am and who I aspire to be. Wanting more for myself and my family. I started taking free online development classes, certifications, and skill training. Learning and growing more during the first phase of the pandemic were my goal. I started to read more about credit restoration and credit relief during the pandemic, knowing that if I restored my credit and level, my credit score would allow me to make better investments, purchase properties, and start a new business. If anything, I learned during these times of uncertainty, we should take advantage of every opportunity before us and seize the moment.

My husband and I started a new business in the trucking industry as an investment for our family legacy. My focus became a little clearer, and many goals and tasks that I wrote out for myself I was able to check off my "bucket list."

I begin sharing my accomplishments with excitement with April, but my excitement wasn't matched by hers. This went on with every accomplishment; the more I was excited the more she become uninterested. One day I asked her simply, "What's wrong?"

April stated, "I am tired of everyone asking me about you as if I can't go anywhere without you."

Baffled, I replied, "Why would that make you upset?"

She said, "And you think everyone likes you; well, they don't because you think you are better than everyone else!"

Now, remember, this is my friend—no, let me rephrase. This is my best friend for over twenty years who decided to take this time to tell me how she really felt. As the conversation progressed, she continued to pour out her feelings. I stopped her in mid-sentence and apologized to her for anything I may have said to hurt her or her feelings.

Again, I asked, "What did I do to upset you?"

She reminded me of the statement I had made several weeks prior, "We are reaching fifty years of age, and we haven't accomplished much or completed the goals we've set for ourselves."

At this moment, I began to think that how she felt was really not about me but about where she was in her life.

There is a 2015 article on Goodnet.org, "The 8 Defining Characteristics of a Best Friend, which lists them listed as:

1. Telepathy: BFFs read you minds before the words pop out your mouth.

2. Honesty: BFFs should give you a real opinion: sometimes it may seem a bit harsh or they may even disagree with your choices. Your best friend won't hide their views.

3. Humor: BFFs find humor in almost any situation.

4. Empathy: Your BFF can actually feel what you are going through.

5. Generosity: Giving is something that comes naturally between best friends.

6. Trust: Your BFF would never use your private information against you or to hurt you in any way.

7. Encouragement: Your BFF always thinks you are awesome.

8. Steadfastness: Your BFF has your back no matter what.

As the days and the weeks went by, the telephone calls, text messages, and visits from April drew slim to none. Each time I tried to reach out, I would get the same reply: "There's nothing wrong, bestie. I'm just working on me." But then I saw her on social media with her newfound friends, doing the things she and I used to do.

During my progression to becoming a better me, I decided to change my environment, my thinking, and even some of the people who were not in alignment with my newness and current journey. Needless to say, my relationship with my "best friend" was dwindling day by day, leaving me in a wondering state because of where she wanted to stay versus where I wanted to be. Each day, I began to feel a void of no longer having April around to share stories, accomplishments, and some "good ole tea" with.

Now weeks turned into months, and every blue moon I'd make the first move to send a text to say, "Hi sunshine, I'm just checking on you," and the reply would always be the same: "Hey, Bestie, I'm good."

One day in conversation with a mutual friend named Lisa, sipping a glass of Chardonnay, Lisa shared that she overheard April saying awful things about me to another friend. Shocked and at a loss for words, I put on a, "Child, I don't care anymore," face to hide the pain and heartbreak for someone I truly cared about and called a best friend. I had to know why these things were said and why were we in this space.

I called April and asked, "How did we get here; what did I do to you?"

Her response was, "Bestie, we're good; stop believing everything you hear; everyone is lying. I didn't say those things," only to find out everything April said to people came with proof.

This has me rethinking the term "best friend" and believing the phrase, "When someone shows you who they are, believe them." During this season I learned to understand the true qualities of a friend, to accept that things don't last forever, and that to prosper during this journey, we have to learn to forgive those who have hurt us and whom we may have hurt as well. That's what friends are for.

My commitment has always been to see everyone win and to encourage them to turn their passion into a profession or benefit. When you decide to make a commitment to better yourself, never feel as though you have to dumb yourself down to make others comfortable in your uncomfortable world. You are unstoppable! Let them play catch up.

COVID-19 has been a trying time for all of us, mentally, physically, emotionally, spiritually, and financially, but it gave us a chance to experience the unexpected and overcome adversity by remaining resilient.

CHAPTER FIVE:

COMPANIONSHIP IN THE MIDDLE OF A PANDEMIC AND IN THE MIDST OF A CRISIS

ALDITH J LOWE

He died on my birthday, December 3, 2019. I was just about to leave the house. I was in my blue, long-sleeved silk shirt with the tie at the wrists and my khaki slacks. I was giving myself a once-over in the mirror. I was about to head out to the hospital to give Patrick Vassell his second massage for the week.

As I turned to look at my butt, my cell phone rang.

The voice on the other end said, "You don't have to go to the hospital again. He's gone. Boss is gone."

I was in shock, and I immediately started to ask questions. That is how I get when I am given bad news. I try to get all the facts in detail so that I can mentally process it. I think my friend was beginning to get overwhelmed with the twenty-one questions I was asking, and so she ended the conversation by saying she had to call others to inform them. I was not yet done with my line of questioning, but I understood that it wasn't an easy task she was engaged in, informing others of his death while she was processing her grief.

I had an appointment at 9:20 a.m. I turned off my phone and went to the car. As I backed out of the driveway, I wasn't sure if I had the strength or mental wherewithal to make the journey to the dentist, but I had to go. I had to keep my mind occupied. I turned off the radio and drove in silence as I really wanted to have a heart-to-heart talk with God. There were moments I heard audible mumblings, and then I would retreat into my head to have further discussions with God.

I realized that I was driving purely on muscle memory because I wasn't really cognizant of what was happening on the road. I just knew I was going somewhere. It was early hours still, so I decided to stop at my happy place until it was time for my appointment. I stopped at the Jamaica Pegasus Hotel. After walking the lawns for however long, I sat in the café and ordered breakfast. I sat in a daze just staring into the abyss of my mind while waiting for my order.

As I ate, I was drawn into the memory of when my mom had passed, that agonizing memory of a day I would rather not remember. I reached into my bag and took out my phone to check the time just to be sure I was not late for my appointment. I realized that the phone was still turned off. After turning on the phone, I received my first birthday call from Dr. Wilson; it was a serenade like no other. I burst out laughing when he said, "I know I can't sing, but I'm glad I could make you laugh." With that, I got up from the table headed to the lady's room, got it together, forced myself to take a few selfies, and headed out to my appointment.

My Hospital Stay

The following Tuesday, December 10, 2019, a memorial was being held in honor of Patrick at work. It was scheduled for 2 p.m. As the time drew closer to 2, I noticed that my heart began to race a little bit more. Sally and I walked over to the lecture theatre. As I got closer. I noticed my heart was beating even faster. As we entered the lecture theatre from the back, the room was packed beyond capacity. I looked through the crowd standing at the back to find the guys from the Printery. I found them and went and stood with them; after all, it was not just the university's loss but also our loss. Boss (as he was affectionately called) was not only the supervisor of the Printery; he was a protector, a brother, a friend, a father figure, and everything wrapped up in one. We were in the back of the lecture theater, and we were just in time to see the pictorial review of his life and the remembrance.

The room was silent as the pictures flashed across the screen, except at various intervals when there were eruptions of laughter. I gripped Sheldon's hand firmly as I started to feel a sharp pain in my chest. I stooped to the ground, not letting go. He turned to ask what was wrong, but I couldn't speak because of the pain I was feeling. He rubbed my hand as the pictorials kept flashing across the screen. As the memorial ended, people began to disperse; some descended the steps, while others left through the back. I stood at the back of the lecture theatre looking down on everyone leaving the room and others gathering to meet with Patrick's widow. I continued to watch as the room became emptier; by this time I was the only one standing at the back of the room. Someone looked up at me from the front and asked if I were OK. I nodded and gave a half-smile, knowing full well that something wasn't right.

As I walked across campus, I could hardly breathe, so I went to the medical center. After arriving, I looked at the nurse, and she beckoned me to come around and sit. Before any words could come out, I started bawling. It was a wailing that I have never heard before. Through the tears, I remember telling her that my friend died, and I hollered. For the first time since my friend died on my birthday, I cried. The nurse placed me in the treatment room as I could not be contained with the amount of hollering I was doing at the front desk. I cried because I was now able to release all the pent-up pressure I was holding because I could not allow myself to feel anything before I did the final part of my stats exam. I cried because I felt sad that my ex-husband lost his uncle three days after I lost my friend. I cried and cried and cried. I went into a frenzy. My friends, Sally and Nadine came from the office, and they rubbed my back and calmed me down. The nurse had asked if I had wanted to see the doctor, but I told her no and that I was fine. I think I just really needed to cry and grieve the loss of my friend.

On the way home, I felt discomfort, but I hoped I could reach the Portmore Medical Complex before it got too bad. I decided not to drive our regular route down Deanery Road, so I turned at the stadium and headed to Marescuax Road. I felt my heart racing, and by this time, I could it feel it ferociously throbbing below my jaw. I stopped right in front of Tom Red Cam Library and left the car. I approached Nadine's car window and told her that I needed to go back up to the office and see the doctor as I wasn't feeling well. We tried calling to see if the doctor were still there. I started to vomit on the side of the road. I could hear a man shout from his car going in the other direction saying, "Yes, you're pregnant!"

Alex, my youngest son, who was by my side, said, "Mom, let's not wait. Let's go now." We got back in the car. I put on my hazard lights and spun the car around and went back in the direction I came from. Nadine was not so rough on the road, and she was a little distance behind. In the moment I felt fear, nervousness, and every emotion that could possibly come in such a time like this.

I did have an adrenaline rush driving through traffic with my hazard lights on; however, the fun of it wasn't being felt as I was more concerned about whether I were going to make it. At one point I couldn't get through the traffic, and Alex got out of the car to ask people to shift because I was in distress. Finally, I arrived at the Accident and Emergency gate. I flew out of the driver's seat and barely spoke to the security person, who put me in a wheelchair and wheeled me in. I don't remember whom I gave the car keys to or what happened to them.

I was wheeled into one of the cubicles where a doctor was sitting on a stool facing some machines. The security calmly said to him, "Doctor, chest pain." He didn't respond but continued to do what he was doing. She again said, "Doctor, chest pain." Although it was in the same calm voice, it was a bit more audible and forceful. He turned and started to question me as doctors do.

I was grabbing my chest. I wanted to throw up, so I beckoned for a bowl. It was a blue bowl, and I vomited. I remember it was red, and the doctor was trying to see if it were blood. I was hooked up to a machine, and my finger was placed in that little thing to see that enough oxygen was getting into my lungs. Again I was throwing up. After they checked my vitals, I was sent to get registered. Of course, I asked what was wrong, but I was only given limited information. I was told that I presented as a heart patient, so all the questions I was asked were geared toward that.

My first hospital stay lasted four days, the first night of which was spent sitting in the A&E waiting room. When I finally got a bed, I stayed in A&E until about midday. My time on the ward was not the most pleasant as I wasn't an easy patient to feed because of my allergies. I survived on fruits and coconut water mainly. During that time, I was on eleven different medications, three of which were for my allergies.

My second hospital stay came two days before New Year's Day. I was feeling chest pains, and after I went to the Portmore Medical Complex, the attending physician sent me straight to the hospital. I spent another two days lying down in the A&E.

The Friendship

Thor (not his real name) and I have been friends for as long as I can remember working at the university. We often volunteered at various university events, such as alumni meetups, Open Day, and Research and Technology Day. I think our favorite spot was the Ganga tree; well, that was my favorite spot. I liked the aroma, only to suffer in the nights from a terrible headache.

After I was released from the hospital, Thor checked on me quite often. It was December 23rd when he visited me. He said I needed to get out of the house. He brought snacks, banana chips, and a bottle of Malta. We sat on the rocks close enough to the sea but far enough away that my allergies wouldn't be triggered. We talked for what seemed like hours, and when it started to get dark, he took me back home. It was a nice gesture, and I had needed to get out of the house.

He began to check on me almost every day, ensuring that I was not worrying and that I was taking my medication. We would talk for hours on end. He had been my statistics tutor the previous semester and so had become a cheerleader for me where it concerned my studies. The transition from cheerleader to on-call doctor's assistant was easy for him.

The university closed on March 12, 2020 as a result of a confirmed COVID-19 case on the island. There were some essential workers who were required to go to work to ensure that the university still remained operational. My unit was scheduled, and each member was required to report to the office at least two days per week. He began to travel with me on the days I went into the office.

We became travel partners. Even on days when he could work from home, he would ensure that he was at work when I was coming to work. On the days we were at work together, we would have lunch after work, comprised mostly of KFC at the park. We sat for hours in the park talking about events in both our lives, procedural and policy matters at work, and possibly how we could improve them. I looked forward to our lunch conversations and our travel time in the mornings and evenings. Our bond of friendship was becoming stronger.

At first, he was a bit reserved, and I was always the one chatting away because he would ask a lot of questions. I didn't mind as it amounted to talk therapy for me. On the days when I didn't see my psychiatrist, he was my on-call therapist of sorts, although I was a little petrified to tell him those deep dark things that haunted me. I remember wondering on numerous occasions why he kept traveling with me and being there for me with no strings attached. I even discussed the matter with a very close friend. I just couldn't understand why he always wants to be around me. My friend laughed so hard at me I was embarrassed. I was getting a little suspicious.

Thor told me about his trip to visit his mother, and I asked that he take me the next time he was going to the country. That trip was one of the most relaxing I've been on in a long time. We stopped by the side of the gorge and actually went over the barrier close to the water. We visited his mom and bought ground provisions in the market. That was the first of quite a few trips to visit his mom and brothers. He was a very private person, so I told him that I appreciated the fact that he brought me into his world.

No matter what was happening at work or in his personal life, he would make sure he came with me to see the doctor. The first time he accompanied me to the cardiologist, after the visit, I lay in the car and cried. He wasn't sure what to do, so he took me to the place where he would go to let off steam; it was near the water. We both discovered that we both loved the water, so next to what is now our favorite jerk food spot, anyplace where there is water is our getaway.

I don't think I had allowed anyone to get this close to me as I always try to dissuade even the thought of anyone being close. But there is a saying that some people come into our lives for a reason, some for a season, and some for a lifetime. I'm not sure which category this friendship will fall into, but I am thankful that during this season of my life, provision has been made for a friend to be by my side throughout the challenges.

CHAPTER SIX:

GRIEVE YOURSELF BACK TO LIFE

KEESHA BARREAU

I have never experienced so many deaths as I did in 2020. Every other day, someone was ringing or texting my phone to let me know that someone had died. It was becoming unbearable. The more they told me the more I felt like I myself was slowly dying. Death was all around me. I did not know what to do or whom to turn to. Death had become a familiar tune, and it was playing in everyone's home. I was beginning to suffer from PTSD. I had just lost my father two years ago and was still going through the stabbing pains of grief. I was reliving the same pain but more intensely. I could not shake it. There were nights when I literally heard myself moaning in my sleep. The sound was coming from the deepest part of me, the place where I stored all my pain. No matter how much I tried, I couldn't stop the tears, so I just let them flow.

I was slowly losing interest in everything. I just wanted to be home with my husband and my son. I was afraid of death, afraid of losing anyone else. I started having anxiety attacks. At night I would check to see if my husband were still breathing. I would run to my son's room to check if he were OK. No book, no sermon, nothing could have prepared me for this kind of pain. I was not OK! Grief was staring me in the face. I was staring back but had no ammunition for it. I was fighting a battle that I was slowly losing. How could I deal?

I was operating in a robotic mode, and I needed to get back to living and not just existing. I prayed night and day, but the only words that I could hear myself saying through the groaning and the tears were, "Help me, God!" I knew the scriptures, but they were not resonating in my spirit. My heart was sad. I was grief stricken. My own insightful words could not comfort me. I needed God's help. I prayed! I cried out to God and asked Him to help me. I told Him I was afraid. I told him I did not understand. I told him that I was mad at him. I told him the pain was too much. I told him everything.

And then He told me to write.

I took a break from social media and began journaling again. Thoughts raced through my mind. I could not be the only one undergoing this painful heart turbulence. I started thinking about all my friends who had lost loved ones. I was not only living with the weight of my own grief, but I also found myself carrying the grief of others, many of whom were still hurting. I knew I had to do something. I determined in my heart that I would use the pain and transform it into something meaningful, something that offered a glimmer of light, a simple guide that would help in navigating through unprepared, unplanned emotional upheaval. I had to find a way to transform the process of grief into hope.

Written from the deepest cavity of my heart that stored all my grief, this is "Grieve Yourself Back to Life!" (This is the part where I ran to the bathroom and bawled my eyes out.)

The Waltz

"Dear life, I was not ready."

Life is definitely a dance: beautiful, fun, smooth, progressive yet risky, with adventurous and flowing movements. However, no matter how we try to choreograph our lives or how much we rehearse, each life has its own course that also comes with dangerous, continuous turns as well as rises and falls. While we are waltzing through life, God presents us with different dance partners who travel with us: mothers, fathers, siblings, spouses, children, and curated friendships. These partners can be here for a long or short while, but no matter the length of time, we create and share unforgettable memories together. These memories are the invisible threads that fuse us together even after death.

Grief comes from a loss, and it is accompanied with great pain and sadness. It is the part of life that we know is inevitable, yet we are never fully prepared for. The devastation that comes with this loss is indescribable. The emotions it generates sometimes cannot be explained while they play out in many different ways. Anger, sadness, fear, anxiety, and other emotions seem to crouch at our doorsteps. Our desire to be alone heightens. We want to run away from, "How are you doing?" and, "How are you feeling?" We begin mastering the art of deflecting, which leads to masking when we should be expressing.

Find a healthy way of releasing those emotions. This is where I recommend crying. I found that crying released my pent-up anguish and allowed my heart to decompress and relax. After my crying episodes, I would always feel better. Crying also opens our heart and mind to receive the next wave of comfort that awaits us, whether it is from other family members, children, friends, pastor, church family, coworkers, a random stranger, or, believe it or not, a pet. God will use anything or anyone to provide comfort to His children. In my case, that was my beautiful son, Mason. I noticed that he noticed me, especially when I was sad. He always had a way of delivering the word of comfort that I needed in that given moment.

Mason, "Mommy, are you sad again?"

Me, "Yes, Mason, mommy is sad."

Mason, "Mommy, are you sad for Grandpa?"

Me, "Yes, baby. I miss him so much."

Mason, "Grandpa is in heaven with Jesus, Mommy. And he's coming back soon. OK, Mommy?"

Me, "OK, baby."

God will reveal Himself to you in unique and tangible ways just like he did for me through Mason.

Take some time to think about the different ways in which God brought you comfort during your season of tears. Now, stop reading and tell Him, "Thank You."

I Need a Moment

Dear onlookers, it is not your responsibility to put a time clock on those who are grieving.

Give me a minute or a thousand minutes; give me a day or a thousand days just to cry. I want to mourn the loss, my loss. I want to weep for my loved one. I want to curl up and cry myself to sleep. I want to reminisce about them and cry some more. Just allow me to grieve in my own time, in my own space, in my own way.

Those are the sentiments of so many of us who have experienced a loss. People should not have to explain why they are still grieving. Grieving is healthy, and we need to take time to do so. Everyone grieves differently and at a different pace. Do not allow anyone to hasten your grieving process. There are no manuals that dictate the time frame for grief; however, while grieving we should also bask in the beautiful memories of all the experiences that we shared with the deceased. Grieving does not mean we forget about the person and bury the memories along with them. Grieving is simply going through the process of the pain that comes with a loss. We have to face it, deal with it, and go through it. However, there is no rush.

Give me a minute to clear my head.

I have just experienced a loss; my loved-one is dead.

Do not stand around waiting for me to heal,

Pray me through this painful time as I continue to grieve.

Keep me in your heart, your prayers, and your thoughts;

Please remember that this was a great loss.

As I walk through the valley of the shadow of death,

I need to come out without any regrets,

And while I'm there all alone I must learn how to be still,

So, I can hear God's voice concerning His will.

Say a prayer for me, not just once or twice.

Keep my name on your lips both day and night.

As I continue to wait patiently for my time of relief,

But until then allow me to weep, allow me to mourn, allow me to grieve.

When My Heart Is Overwhelmed

Dear heart, please don't fail me now.

Grief takes us to a place of loneliness and despair. Hopelessness tries to keep us there. It is a real emotion. My body was feeling the weight of my grief, and I had to fight through it. Some days I was winning, and other days grief overwhelmed me. I was tearfully subdued by grief. But I was determined to take each moment in stride and to acknowledge my victories as well as my defeats.

Learn to be in the moment. Whatever it is that you are feeling or experiencing now, acknowledge it. When we disregard our feelings, we do more damage than good. We must walk in our own truth. Truth of how we are feeling. Sometimes the answer to our truth does not reveal itself the same day, and this is where patience comes in. We have to learn to be patient with ourselves to teach others how to be patient with us. Healing is not an overnight thing. Sometimes it takes longer than we would like. Offer yourself the grace you need and continue your journey toward hope.

It is OK to ask "Why?" Go ahead and ask.

Good Morning, Sunshine!

Dear light, I see you piecing through.

There is a greater emotion that overrides grief if we make room for it. That emotion is hope. Hope gives us something to look forward to, something to work toward. Hope replaces despair and causes our heart to leap with possibilities. The belief that each day gets better and that we will smile again is within reach. Having the right people around to encourage us through our grieving process will also help us get there.

My heart broke again when the 2020 deaths came rolling in. And once again, my husband was right there to ensure that my broken heart did not shatter into irreparable pieces. He covered me with his love and his presence. He allowed me to grieve; he grieved with me. He made sure that grief did not consume me. He cradled my heart with delicacy and precision. He knew I was fragile, and so he became my physical blanket of comfort and care.

A great recipe for healing through grief is having people around who will be in the trenches of grief with us. They know the right ingredient to offer in the moment that it is needed. That person has to be able to offer many emotions (e.g., compassion, kindness, silence, consideration, understanding, tenderhearted, sympathy, empathy, reality, encouragement) and switch out accordingly. Then at some point we will have to decide whether or not we wish to stay buried and overcome by grief or choose to bask in the memories that we have of the ones we lost.

Even though our loved ones are no longer with us, memories of them can strengthen us and carry us through the remainder of our life's journey. That's something that death will never be able to take away.

Now, place one foot in front of the other, rise up from your ashes of grief, and face the new day. There are new people to meet and new memories to create. "Weeping may endure for a night, but joy comes in the morning" (Psalm 30:5).

You can take everything but my memories,
for they're good ones and they'll see me through.
If we never meet again, I'll love you forever,
I'll leave this world loving you.—Wayne Kemp

(Dedicated to my daddy Ivan Emmanuel Maitland and all the beautiful souls that we lost in 2020.)

CHAPTER SEVEN:
HEALING LESSONS FROM COVID-19

JAMES STEWARD

The COVID-19 pandemic forever changed the world in 2020 and consequently the ministry of pastoral care. To that end, we in ministry must be intentional about faithfully responding to God's call in this global challenge. We play a critical role in ministry during these unprecedented times. It is my objective to present this story as a call to arms toward reaffirming our ministry with others in the age of COVID-19.

Let me offer a brief background about myself. I serve in congregational ministry as a lead pastor, professor, and clinical pastoral education supervisor in the New York City area. My life and work experiences have given me many insights into ministry, which inevitably influences these lessons.

I have spent about fifteen years in ministry as a pastor, an educator, an administrator, and clinician. During that time, I have cared for families who did not get the chance to say goodbye to their loved ones and those who did. Have you ever loss something or someone that you didn't have a chance to say goodbye to? One of my biggest lessons from COVID-19 was the impact of complicated grief. When we can't grieve a loss entirely, it leaves an enormous hole. Saying goodbye begins the healing process!

At the beginning of the COVID-19 pandemic, I spent the majority of my clinical work FaceTiming families who could not visit their loved ones in the hospital due to COVID-19 restrictions. I often held up my iPad or phone to a dying patient's ear as, one by one, family members said their final goodbyes before they passed from this life. While a family's grief was palpable, there was gratefulness as they expressed to me how valuable my doing this small thing was for them. This is one of many lessons I have learned as a pastoral caregiver in the middle of a pandemic. Being a pastor, clinical chaplain, and administrator is already an intense, daily learning experience. By early 2020, it evolved into an education I never thought I would experience. I have discovered, rediscovered, and had affirmed an abundance of lessons that are worth sharing outside of the hospital setting as it relates to COVID-19. For people that I ministered to, I let them shout about the injustice of this virus. While we tend to repress things as human beings, shouting is often cathartic.

Additionally, another lesson I learned is that laughter is a sign of healing and life. This virus is cruel and deadly. But we still need laughter for release as it reminds us that joy is still possible even until the end. Laughter does not negate the pain and suffering people are enduring, but it reminds us that life can still have joy. We have often heard that it is OK to get angry. And that proved to be another lesson of COVID-19. Anger is a grief response. During COVID-19, I witnessed members, students, patients, families, and health care staff in anger. But rather than distract them from it or tell them a theological cliché like, "This, too, shall pass," I invited people to explore and express that anger. That is what ministry is about, to be able to journey with people in the midst of their circumstances.

The catchphrase for COVID-19 has been, "We're in this together," and we really are in this together. We were witnessing real isolation but know that even for patients intubated and alone in a hospital room, it is by working together that we able to care for and even heal these patients. We may be isolated, but we still need each another. I have directly experienced the effects of this in a hospital setting and indirectly from my church members virtually. Self-quarantining and social distancing are altruism at its finest.

COVID-19 and Its Effect on Ministry

I do not know of anyone who prepared for a global pandemic in 2020, and certainly I didn't. However, the way we've done ministry in the past must be recalibrated to meet the needs of the times. This is especially true as we deal with our own anxiety and trauma alongside those we are providing care for in the face of this pandemic. From being on the front lines during this coronavirus pandemic, I realized that we are first responders. We may not play a role in the healing of the bodies of our patients, but we play an essential role in caring for their souls as they go through the death and dying process.

What is so important to humanity is connection. But in the case of COVID-19, quarantining has required us to connect in other ways. We have come up with incredibly imaginative ways over time to find connections even when we're not in the same physical space together. However, one can argue that this only creates the illusion of connection. Patients who come to the hospital are typically surrounded by loved ones, which usually brings peace to both them and their families. But during this pandemic, patients find themselves alone in the hospital setting because of health care regulations. Seeing this change has reiterated to me how we are created by God to be in community and communion with each other, especially in a journey of suffering like COVID-19.

As time goes along, the impact of this pandemic may forever change things from the way we conduct our worship services, to how we teach our students, to how we provide pastoral care to grieving families. We may not be able in many cases to sit at the bedside of a patient or family and hold their hands while engaging in meaningful conversation with them. In pastoral care, this is a tradition that originated as a sign of trust but is now one of the most common ways of transmitting the virus. There is nothing normal about some of the things we do anymore. It is the proverbial new normal.

How Ministry Changed

As this age of COVID-19 and racial unrest continue, pastors will continue to play a critical role in the emotional and pastoral support of people. As always, we are called upon to be companions to others and journey alongside those who are suffering.

I.   Adapting Is More Important than Ever

Being adaptive in the face of change is a core tenet of ministry. Experiencing COVID-19's effects has put on full display experiential learning for me. As a congregational pastor, I've seen the impact on my church building closing and how it has necessitated doing virtual church services and electronic ministry to my congregation. As a clinical chaplain, I visited patients at the bedside as they were dying, but many of us have not. Instead, we've been relegated to tele-chaplaincy.

COVID-19 has increased the need for us to strategize how to do creative ministry in the midst of pandemic constraints. Many of us have shifted from automatic in-person visits to all patients to strategies using phone and videoconferencing technologies. Telephones, videoconferences, and the like are not new, but many who had formerly dismissed such technology have come quickly to learn its usefulness. For many of us, the pandemic has invited us to question again the primacy of physical presence in our work.

II.   Recalibrating What We Know as "Ministry of Presence"

As pastoral caregivers, we know the importance of the ministry of presence in our work. We are called to ministry largely because it is so profoundly meaningful to be present with others in major crises and journey with them. Being present with others is at the heart of what we do in ministry. However, COVID-19 presents us with a different kind of challenge. And there seems to be an increased vulnerability and connection by being creative in connecting to people like never before.

Despite our ability in 2020 to have video conferencing, telephones, live streaming, and the like, there's nothing like being around people physically. There is a fundamental challenge to ministry when the assembly cannot assemble. Pastoral care done virtually, while effective is not the same as in person. In my career in ministry, I've experienced death and dying, but this pandemic is a whole new reality. Maybe it's because it's challenging and unnatural to grieve in isolation. But I've actually found that in many ways, this may be the best ministry I have ever done. The creativity in retooling that many of us had to do to meet the needs of the current moment in the midst of this crisis is remarkable in many ways. I leave you this call to be intentional about finding ways to faithfully respond to God's call to showing up for others and journeying with people in love, empathy, and compassion. For doing this, we are being the hands and feet of Christ in a broken world so loved by God.

CHAPTER EIGHT:

HIS GRACE IS SUFFICIENT FOR ME—GOD CAN BLESS YOU IN ANY SEASON!

DIANA SHARPE

We arrived in Calgary, Alberta from Regina on Friday, March 6, 2020, they had fewer than ten COVID-19 cases, and Regina had none. COVID-19 was a new buzz word in the Western world, but I had been following the news closely in China and the East for a few months, and I had seen the despair, devastation, and death on the news, and I knew this was serious. I had prayed earnestly that it would not come to our shores, but alas, it did.

It was Monday, March 9, 2020. I had just returned from a fiery weekend of church services in Calgary. I was coughing, sneezing, and aching all over. I pushed past my feelings and went to work because we had an open house to showcase our program to prospective students; in hindsight, this decision was foolish. I kept a reasonably safe distance from the students I interacted with, but I knew enough even then that staying home would have been best. I recovered after a few days and was told by the health line that I didn't have the symptoms of the dreaded virus, so I escaped taking the test. I am grateful that that one mistake was not a deadly one for me or anyone else.

On Friday, March 13, things began to shut down, and our campus shifted to virtual learning, which was a revolting, sudden, and difficult shift for students, faculty, and staff. Students were quickly pulled from clinical settings as we waited to learn more about this virus and awaited further instructions from the Health Authority. In the short-term, students were not being allowed in hospital units or long-term care facilities.

The world had come to standstill just as many of us were getting ready to unveil big plans of grandeur and purpose. I had many personal, professional, and entrepreneurial endeavors that I had planned to execute during the year. With everything grinding to a halt, I took a minute to think, pivot (Everybody was using this word. I am throwing it in here for humor.), and reposition myself and my business. This minute lasted for two months and saw me cooking and baking up a storm daily. I posted daily on Facebook and tantalized the visual senses of my family and friends. I freely shared recipes, instructions, and baked goods. I even sold some cornbread, Easter buns, and banana bread, but I did this more out of love than profit. I was happy, and I was feeling a sense of satisfaction, but I knew there was more work to be done, and this was merely a distraction, albeit a good one. My waistline was also telling one story, and my bank account was telling another; they were quickly becoming polar opposites and enemies, and so I slowed it down.

I work as an academic advisor at one of the two universities in my city, and I tutor and coach elementary and high school students with a private company that offers in-home services. Together, both jobs and my occasional, now-consistent coaching clients afford me a decent living. Back in March, I had five students; we quickly offered to shift our lessons to online, but some parents and students were not able to adjust to this new normal. At the end of March, I only had two students; this resulted in a significant decline in my income. There were moments when I was concerned, but I held on. I knew that God's grace was and continues to be sufficient for me. I did not qualify for the government COVID-19 assistance for persons who had lost all or most of their income, and there was a stubborn, industrial, and independent streak within me that didn't want me to apply for any assistance. There is nothing wrong with applying for assistance when truly needed, but I still had my day job, and I didn't want to take a "gift" that I would have to repay next year. So, I dusted off my goals and planning book, and I got to

Over the next few months, I would transform my life one small action at a time. I have been writing my autobiography for almost ten years, and during spurts of self-discipline and passion, I would write a chapter or two, and then I would put it aside. In the middle of COVID-19, people were searching for hope, and Dr. Joan Wright-Good was happy to share a little hope with her community, so she invited a group of us to share a paragraph from a book we had read. I had many books laying around, but my favorite story is my own, so I read a chapter from my unpublished autobiography, "Why Can't We Take the Bus?" Everyone loved it, and I knew I had to get back to writing. I am now writing more consistently and have finally settled into a routine of writing at least once a week. My publishing goal date is 2021; friends will hold me to it.

There were several other pending tasks that I knew I had to get done, so I kept my focus. My savings were dwindling, the country was on shut down for what seemed an indefinite time, but the scripture reminded me that His grace was sufficient for me, so I was hopeful. I had dreams of taking my Women's Empowerment event to three cities in 2020, an overly ambitious and costly dream, but a girl can and should dream! My first event attracted twenty participants, and I made extraordinarily little money, but I had gained so much more than money could buy. I had gained God-fidence (confidence inspired by God). I gained new clients and a small mailing list (important for future events). I had more clarity and organization around my business and the services that I wanted to offer. More important, I gained a new sense of direction and purpose. I wanted to empower women worldwide, and I was ready to get this show on the road but for COVID-19.

After a few months, I recognized that in-person events would not be a reality in 2020, so I created a revised plan, a virtual global conference. I soon realized that there was value and opportunities in going virtual; the event would be bigger and better. There were indeed blessings and good things happening even in the pandemic, but there was one issue. I could not contact the person that I had selected to be my primary speaker. For two months, I texted, emailed, and left messages with no answer; finally, I prayed, "Lord, I (emphasis on the I) want her to speak, but is this Your will? And if it is, let her return my call, Amen." The next day, I got a call and an apology.

That call shifted my summer and the rest of my year. It wasn't just the fact that the speaker had said yes; it was that God said yes. I sprang into action ordering banners, creating my participants' workbook with my accountability partner who has some great design and arrangement skills, setting up my Instagram account, and ordering my Empowerment Tees. The story around my empowerment t-shirt line is a very interesting one. In 2019 when the spirit of God gave me my event idea, I was also inspired to create a t-shirt line that shared the messages of the event and bore simple empowering slogans. In 2019, when most people had jobs and some had a reasonable disposable income, I feared no one would support my business, so I held back on the T-shirts. I listened to the noise in my head and from a few persons around me, and I incorrectly assumed that no one would buy my t-shirts. The voices screamed, "They can't afford it. They don't need it."

I discovered that was not true. In a pandemic, I have sold more than seventy t-shirts and have shipped t-shirts to Jamaica, Florida, Boston, London, and even Japan. I saw my clients as coming from my church circle (seventy-five people), maybe my city (300,000 people). My lenses were limited and small; now I know beyond a shadow of doubt that my circle is the world. Yes, "The earth is the Lord's, and the fullness thereof; the world, and they that dwell therein" (Psalm 24:1). Matthew 6 reminds us that if He takes cares of the bird of the air, how much more for us who are more valuable and loved by Him? Not only did my people support me, but many purchased repeatedly. Stock was sold out repeatedly, and the local community that I once doubted showed up and showed off.

I must also share that a friend planted the seed for my t-shirt business, based on a single prayer I prayed to God. The deposit for the t-shirt order was due on a Friday, and payday was the next Monday. I told the supplier I would transfer the payment on Monday, and he settled for the three-day delay. On Sunday as I left church, my best friend messaged, "Please check your email." I looked, and there was an e-transfer for $300, the exact amount I had prayed about. I screamed for joy and broke out in tears. God heard my prayer, and He provided just what I needed. I want someone to know that God's grace is sufficient to keep you, even in a pandemic.

In a pandemic I created, launched, and achieved the following:

1. Hosted my first Global Women's Empowerment conference with more than a hundred attendees from more than six countries and made a profit

2. My first paid consultation project. (It wasn't a thousand in one day, but it was a couple thousand in a few days! I am forever grateful, and my goal is to deliver, repeat, deliver, repeat.)

3. My Empowerment Tee-shirt (The line sold out multiple times and is now available on my website with new designs and slogans.)

4. Started a baking side hustle.

5. YouTube channel youtube.com/
   watch?v=f5tjYhrH6Zg&t=22s

6. Podcast channel about women with inspiring stories: Dee
   Sharpe Thoughts, now available on my website, Anchor,
   Spotify, Apple, and my YouTube channel

7. Website: deesharpethoughts.com

8. Resumed writing (This is major. This writing project was
   another good kick-start.)

9. Getting ready to launch my own education service
   company

10. Started school (The course is amazing. This course
    affirms that I have found my thing, my why, my passion.
    I want to continue working with youth and women,
    and this course helps me to gain new skills to help both
    groups. Please read my second submission to hear about
    that experience and to gain inspiration for dealing with
    children who exhibit challenging behavior.)

How did I do it? I am happy you asked.

I got paid coaching, training, and mentoring to enhance
my coaching, mentoring, podcast/YouTube, and entrepreneurial
skills during the two months that I took a break. There are a
lot of free courses and amazing podcasts about starting a digital
business, a multi-media business, a baking business, a podcast;

whatever you need, it is out there. I got an accountability partner who was more like a drill sergeant. She has great administrative, time management, planning, and execution skills. She knows how to get the job, and she helped me stay on track. I also set clear and precise goals and objectives with firm deadlines; my accountability partner ensured that I did not miss a beat. I closely followed and engaged with people on social media and in my community, who were producing, executing, and thriving in the face of everything happening around them. I prayed daily for God's guidance, direction, and will.

Finally, I got started. It is as simple as that. I got started in my state of incompleteness, imperfection, doubt, fears. I got started. As Zig Ziglar said, "You don't have to be great to start, but you have to start to be great." If you wait for perfection, you will never start since perfection eludes all of us.

I started my YouTube channel by simply switching my profile from private to public (So many people have asked how; it is that simple.) and began recording videos using my Samsung S7 and about ten textbooks as my Tripod. I would have to rush to complete filming by 5 p.m. since my basement suite was poorly lit, and I had no ring light. I later invested in a $7 ring light from Walmart and a $19 Tripod, which barely did the job, but I kept going. I have since upgraded to a USB fine microphone, Sony noise cancelling headphones, ring light with a proper stand, new laptop, and a host of other upgrades. My assistant who assists with my editing has since advised that in another two months he would like me to invest into new equipment and a more professional studio look. I am all for it and will be implementing those changes. I am all about delivering the best product and improving my craft.

For my virtual event, I hired three speakers before I even sold my first ticket. I trusted God to help me cover the speaker fees, and He did.

To gain my client (the paid consultation), I simply checked in with a professional whom I had worked with in the past and inquired how he was doing. When he shared he had a problem, I was happy to provide the solution. The biggest take away from that consultation was that you do not need to know everything to make a significant impact in a client's life or business.

I achieved these goals and milestones through hard work, hours of studying, tears, sweat, and my own investment of time and money, but most importantly, I did it by the grace of God! Truly His grace is sufficient for me and you, and He is able to bless us in all seasons!

Life is not without lessons, and 2020 has given us our fair share. As I shared in episode 1 of my podcast, my life's journey and 2020 in particular has taught me that:

- There are blue skies after storms.

- It's important to bring your own sunshine.

- You have to turn your own wheel.

- I am my own safety net, and my goal is to build a strong net.

- God's grace is sufficient to keep me, and He feeds His children spiritual and material manna even in the desert, even in a drought, and even in a pandemic. When everything around you is falling apart, God's grace will help you keep it together. So, be encouraged, keep praying, sowing, going, and growing. You will be amazed at the beauty that awaits you on the other side.

If you have been in a similar position of feeling stuck, doubting yourself and your community, and have money-making ideas buried under dust, doubt, and fear, and you feel we would work well together, please send me an email at dssharpe2013@gmail.com or book a discovery call on my website, deesharpethoughts.com.

CHAPTER NINE:

UNPRECEDENTED TIMES CALL FOR UNPRECEDENTED PARTNERSHIPS

SHEDLY CASSEUS-PARNTHER

One of my favorite quotes mentions how opportunities of a lifetime only last within the lifetime of the opportunity. To all my fellow educators of the world, I am positive that you can share my sentiments when I say that the 2020 COVID-19 pandemic created multiple levels of unacceptable inequities amongst our unrepresented, low income, underserved, first-generation families with unmet needs.

Educating students on the college planning and financial aid process was one of my most cherished, gratifying, and invaluable experiences until the unimaginable happened. One week students were excited to spend spring break on a college tour that their families have been saving for an entire year for them to attend, or even spending time completing their college planning tasks, or more commonly planning to work extra hours at a part time job to save for their senior prom and expenses during the break. The very following week those plans were gone because the entire school system shut down, the county shut down, and the state shut down. It was a nightmare that we could not wake up from. As anxiety rose, the abuse at home rose, the hunger within the household rose, depression rose, and the daily educational escapes in which a large number of those students with unmet household needs were gone because the entire country shut down—well, almost.

"Almost" because not all student needs went unmet: not all students had an issue with internet access or technological barriers, not all students had a new experience with virtual learning, not all students had to share a space with two or three of their siblings in one room where they could not focus on the lesson. Has anyone thought about why they were on mute and didn't respond? There was a reason why they didn't show their faces on the school-issued laptop cameras? Not all students have the opportunity; not all students are educated equally.

For once we found ourselves in a space where there were more young voices with questions than educators, adults often known as confidants, had answers for. In a time when our most disadvantaged students were already behind academically and technologically and surrounded by unsurmountable barriers to their post-secondary options, how do we make this work? How does this even happen?

Class of 2020's financial aid and college enrollment numbers plummeted. Everything we had done to bring hope in preparation for an amazing new year was gone. Mental health started to become the priority as the suicide-attempt rates rose. Every single student who could identify as a class of 2020 graduate was affected more so than any other student in the educational system. Preschoolers who dreamt of their first day in kindergarten, the fifth grader who dreamt of their first day in middle school, the eighth grader who looked forward to their first day in high school, and the senior who not only looked forward to grad night and prom and all the student athletes who anticipated their senior nights, their recruiting careers, and their last high school games to later prepare for the first day of college: the Class of 2020 across the board needed great support during these times.

With this in mind, celebrities and moguls around the world virtually joined forces to support the Class of 2020, but what happens when all the virtual support is gone? The where, who, what, and when questions are still left unanswered.

Unprecedented times call for unprecedented partnerships.

A truth that lives in my mind is that unprecedented times call for unprecedented partnerships; a colleague of mine described it so well. Thank you, Yvonne Green; that was powerful in so many ways, and it will live on and be applied forever. As we worked through the tumultuous effects of COVID-19 on our students, we continued to brainstorm on what we were going to do next to support our students. It was time to act because, before we knew it, the Class of 2021 would be caught in the same predicament. It is unacceptable to allow our students to start believing that a post-secondary education is not the first option after high school.

Calling on all willing hands on deck, things have to be put in place: awareness of the vulnerable and the accessibility of the valuable vehicles that need to be in place to be at attention for the deserving students who needed a breath of hope that this is not the end for them and that they still had a chance to experience the life that they have always dreamt of having. All hands on deck! Bring in the front line educators with the political educators who are making the decisions and the policies. Something has to give. It's one thing to publicize the need, and it's another to act.

Our students are being left behind as the rest of the world and technology unapologetically moves forward.

As we find ways to increase the lifetime of the opportunities for the advantage of the disadvantage, the opportunities of a lifetime consistently decrease. Playing catch-up stops feeling like catch-up and starts feeling like running in a hamster wheel. So, they will always be playing catch-up. The unrepresented, low-income, underserved, first-generation families with unmet needs are already deficient in several of the most fundamental subjects needed to obtain promising careers. So, what exactly do you think was happening during the pandemic?

There was a brief period where I felt sick, empty, and hopeless. How could I be in such a position of power and feel so weak? Our jobs are to ensure the educational security of our students, and here I was feeling helpless. What could I do to help? And then it became clear that it is almost impossible to put 100 percent into two initiatives that you love at the same time.

These are our students! They are our future. I don't need the research to confirm that when a student has hope and a plan for their future, the chances of their turning to a life of crime after high school decreases.

It is always our business when it comes to our students! Parents, this is a call to action. Situations such as the COVID-19 pandemic have forced us to prepare our children for unforeseen challenges, which is an experience that is needed to survive in college. Make this a teachable moment to help them persevere and fight for themselves. Help them be self-sufficient and self-motivated to bet on "themselves" because they are enough, and they are worth fighting for. If we don't believe in our youth enough to invest in their growth and their resiliency, how can we expect them to continue to believe in themselves?

Unprecedented times call for our guardians, parents, and educators to start teaching our students to fight differently for a better education and better life.

PART 2

CHAPTER TEN:

FEAR IS NOT YOUR PORTION

MARVA BOZEMAN

As I sat and watched the news from my office computer, I was shocked. It was the middle of March, and all I kept seeing on my computer screen was the word "pandemic." I felt as if we were in a movie, but this was real. My job temporarily closed as I watched the events unfold from home. I was scared. I was scared for my one-year-old daughter and my husband, who suffered from a traumatic brain injury (TBI). I was afraid that my husband or my daughter could be diagnosed with COVID-19. While I relaxed when I learned children were not as affected as adults, the fear remained. What rang in my ear was "people with underlying conditions." All I thought about was my husband. Physical stress or lack of sleep already puts him at risk of a seizure because of the TBI. COVID-19 is not something I wanted him to experience, not when the news was saying people with underlying conditions were dying. Fear became tangible and reminded me of the first time I wrestled with the thought of losing my husband.

I remember it like it happened yesterday. I was seven or eight months pregnant. My husband, Robert, and I were driving home after a long afternoon at church. I turned to glance at Robert and suddenly panicked. I looked at my husband and thought he was having a stroke. His face scrunched upwards instead of drooping on one side. His hand seemed to distort, almost stuck in one position. "Babe! Do you want me to call 911?"

Robert answered me clearly, "No, I'm OK."

I did not see someone who was "OK." I saw someone in need of medical attention. Yet I still didn't know what to do. I saw Robert's face and hands contorted. He wasn't shaking. He wasn't having a seizure. But something was not right. I kept turning my head to look at Robert and back at the road to drive. Thank God traffic was light. My heart was racing, and I was scared. Yet as soon as it had happened, it went away. What lasted a little under a minute seemed like a life time. Just like that, Robert was OK, but I was not.

Tears began to stream down my face. Somehow, I managed to drive despite the blurriness created by sobbing uncontrollably. I remember Robert grabbing my hand to console me. "Babe, I told you this could happen."

I responded, still crying, "Not like that!"

He replied, "Babe, I'm OK. Calm down,"

I cried and cried and cried. I knew we would deal with a medical emergency at some point in our marriage, but not so soon. I managed to stop crying for the duration of our drive home. Robert was OK while I tried to maintain my composure. This was the first-time fear began to torment me as a married woman and soon-to-be mother. Here I was pregnant with our daughter and afraid of what could happen to my husband.

Fear dangled "life" in front of my eyes then, and it dangled "life" in front of my eyes as COVID-19 invaded homes across the world. The fragility of Robert's life was always on my mind. It reminded me of the second time I thought he would lose his life.

It was a few days after my daughter was born. She entered the world on January 1, 2019 and changed both of our lives. We were thrilled yet exhausted. Abra-Rose Faith Bozeman arrived at 10:52 p.m. on Tuesday. We came home from the birth center between 3:30 a.m. and 4 a.m. I put Abra-Rose in her bassinet and carefully climbed into bed, still sore from labor and delivery. Abra-Rose slept four to five hours before she woke up. From there, the newborn cycle began. Most fathers take at least a week or two off work when a child is born. Robert returned Wednesday evening to his night shift from 3 p.m. to 11 p.m. He was barely sleeping as we adjusted to our new schedule. Robert chose not to take time off because of the pressure of my being on maternity leave. I disagreed, but it was what he wanted to do. Our first night home was OK. Wednesday night was fine, but Thursday night proved to be complicated. Abra-Rose was crying and was hard to settle. After a few hours of sleep, she woke up crying, and as new parents, we did not know what to do. My mom helped us out and took the baby into the living room to get some sleep. In hindsight, this was the night that broke that camel's back.

Friday morning came, and we both woke up exhausted. Robert and I sat on the bed, talking to each other. I turned my head, and as quick as I turned back to look at him, Robert was having a seizure. He was on his side, violently shaking. His eyes seemed to roll back, and he was making a strange sound that is hard to describe. I screamed, "Robert! Babe! Mom!" Tears instantly rolled down my face. "Mom!" I grabbed my phone as my fingers fumbled. I dialed 911 and could barely speak. Here I was, barely three days postpartum, and my husband was having a seizure.

All I could think of was death. The 911 operator came on the line and began to take my information. By that time, the shaking stopped, and Robert was in a deep sleep and snoring. That scared me even worse. Was he in a coma? I never caught the operator's name, but I knew God was working through her. She managed to calm me down and explain why my husband was sleeping strangely. The EMT's arrived within minutes and gave Robert oxygen. He began to wake up slowly, but his speech was incoherent. After they administered more oxygen, he was fine. I looked at my mom, holding my baby. Tears were still rolling down my face. My mom reassured me that Robert was fine. Her medical training from her college days plus special education training required her to know what to do in this exact situation.

I think of that day often. Fear tried to grab hold of me. For a while, it succeeded. Seeing my husband have a seizure was one of the scariest moments of my life. Fear shot arrows of death at my mind at every possible moment. *"Marva, Robert's going to eventually die. You'll be a new mom and a young widow."* I secretly cried all the time. For at least two weeks, I would wake up to make sure Robert was OK. Anytime the bed would shake or he would turn in his sleep, I would wake up. I felt tormented. On top of dealing with everything a new mom must face, this caught me off guard. Battling with the added worry of COVID-19 also caught me off guard. What would happen if Robert had a seizure while sick? What would I do? What if the baby saw it? How would she react? Unfortunately, the fear of another seizure became a reality.

The last time it happened was a few months after COVID-19. Like millions of other people, Robert was not working. I was not teaching a full load of classes because it was the summer semester. Both of our schedules were light. There was nothing else in our daily activities that would prepare me for what would happen on that Friday morning in June. I woke up around 5:30 a.m. to Robert violently shaking next to me. It was happening again. I was confused. I did not understand why he was having a seizure. We were taking walks every day. He was not stressed or overworked. Abra-Rose was in bed with us, and so I moved her out of the way. I fumbled as I called 911. My fingers were shaking. I was scared for my husband, and I was afraid for my daughter.

The emergency operator took my information. I assumed it would be a maximum of five minutes before EMT arrived. It took more like ten to fifteen minutes. I sent a text message to my immediate family to let them know I'd be bringing the baby over before I went to the hospital. Simultaneously, I kept asking the operator what was taking so long. My heart started racing. When our daughter was born, Robert quickly came out of the seizure. This one was different. He remained in a deep sleep and wouldn't respond. Where were the first responders when I needed them the most? Abra-Rose was now awake and staring at her dad. I forced myself to keep my composure. I was no good to Robert or her if I fell apart.

The EMTs finally arrived. They began to assist Robert and gave him oxygen. His response was slower than expected. It was a couple of minutes before he started to respond and open his eyes. His movement and speech were slow. My heart was now racing. The EMTs decided to take him to the hospital because they were not comfortable with his response. I grabbed the baby, dropped her off at my parents' home, and met Robert at the hospital. By the time I arrived, he was awake and back to normal. I exhaled. He was OK.

One of the acronyms for fear is "false evidence appearing real." But what do you do when the evidence is real? Then what? What is your response when fear uses factual events against you? Yes, my husband is a gun-shot survivor. Yes, he is vulnerable to seizures, and he battles with lingering effects of the TBI. This is not something that could happen; it did happen. And it could happen again. Fighting fear before COVID-19 was hard. Fighting fear during COVID-19 has been difficult. I felt as if fear had extra ammunition. *"Do you really think Robert could survive COVID-19? A normal person, yes, but not Robert. What if you become a widow?"*

I am learning fear is powerless when I walk in the power of God. I have always 'known' this but now on a deeper level. I sing the songs at church. I declare 2 Timothy 1:7 over my family. I know we should not welcome fear in our lives. But why is the battle so intense? It is because fear wants to control. It wants to rule and reign. It wants me to live in constant fear, always looking over my shoulder to see if Robert is having a seizure or just tossing and turning at night. It wants me to take on anxiety as a false blanket of comfort, manage flare-ups, and call it my own. But God has not given me a spirit of fear. And if God did not give it, then why welcome it? No matter what my physical eyes may behold, I find rest in Psalms 23: 4, "Even though I walk through the valley of the shadow of death, I will fear no evil, for you are with me; your rod and your staff, they comfort me." Whether it's another seizure, unemployment, or even death, fear is not my portion.

CHAPTER ELEVEN:

THEY SAY THAT 2020 IS PERFECT VISION; IS IT?

PETULA BARCLAY

"Way maker, miracle worker, promise keeper, light in the darkness, my God that is Who You are." These are the words from a well-known song, "Way Maker," by African singer Sinach. I found myself singing that song quite often early in January 2020. Little did I know that in a few weeks the words of this song would begin to manifest in my life.

My daughter was in pre-K at the time, doing well academically, and I thought it would be best for her to do her final year at the same preschool and not move her to any other school. So, in February I registered her early for the 2020/2021 school year.

Up to this point, I kept hearing news of a virus outbreak called the Coronavirus (aka COVID-19) in China and other parts of the world. This is a virus that affects/attacks your respiratory system with side effects on other organs of your body, and it's worse if you have an underlying illness. While I was concerned for the people in those parts of the world, I did not put too much thought into it as I figured it would never get to us in every sense of the word: US (the United States, us (my daughter and I), or just us as a people.

Then came March 2020, and my office sent the first emails about the virus, updating us on what was happening locally and internationally: business decisions for other offices we have in different states, stay at home orders, curfews/shutdowns, travel suspensions, and implications for the real estate industry. At this point, I remember thinking that this was getting extraordinarily serious. Terms such as, "We are in this together," and the "new way of living," "new normal," and "crisis management team" suddenly became part of our everyday language. Never have I ever experienced a time such as this or even close to this. I have read and heard about similar times in the past but never thought it would be that way again in my lifetime.

By the second week of March, we were in full COVID-19 operation mode adhering to the local guidelines and CDC rules and regulations. As the days and weeks progressed, it got increasingly challenging to operate in the space I knew and understood as normal. Everything changed rapidly; suddenly school was closed, and my five-year-old daughter needed to do school online. This time also meant that certain business decisions were being made to furlough employees, do salary reduction, and have reduced hours if you were selected to remain on staff.

This was when my faith in God was tested again. It was the beginning of my walk with God down memory lane again. It was also the time that God humbled me and reminded me that He was, is, and will always be enough again. As a single mom, I had grave concerns about what this new normal would be for us. I was concerned about a number of things: my ability to care for my daughter if I lost my job, the safety and well-being of my family and friends near and far, the impact on my bills, the US economy, and the rippled effects of a pre- and post-COVID economy. As I went through a series of, "what-if's," I found myself beginning to doubt that God can or will be able to supply all my needs with all the uncertainties, but God was about to show me His first favor that would leave me frozen.

I work for a prominent real estate company, and my office was officially now closed to the general public. The 200+ agents were asked to work from home and only go to the office briefly to do simple administrative things and leave. Within the first week of the of closure, I religiously went to the office every day for a while to do certain office functions and be a presence for the few who came and left. One of my coworkers was on vacation at the time, so she took the second week upon her return. My other coworkers worked from home. Together with our managers, we kept the office functioning.

The challenge of working from home while trying to do online schooling four to three days of the week with my five-year-old daughter was a huge task. I was not the parent to leave learning 100 percent up to teachers. I was that hands-on parent. I believe every child must learn and will learn when parents take responsibility, partner with teachers, and play a part in the development of their child. By this time, we were in April, and the announcement came that there would be furloughs, salary cuts, and hour reductions. After one of our many town hall meetings with the president, I got a call, and the update was that only two members of staff would remain and work with one manager. I was selected as one of the employees to remain on staff. This was God's first reminder that He is a promise keeper. After the telephone conversation, I wept. I cried for those who would be furloughed, and I cried because I doubted God, and here He was keeping His promise to never leave me, that He will provide, and more important, a reminder that He is my source and all I need.

As the days and weeks passed, the intensity of working from home while doing online school with my daughter got increasingly challenging to balance. I was grateful for the opportunity to still have work during the pandemic, but the weight of the balancing act was real. I was not new to hard and challenging times, but it was during this summer's hurricane season that my home air conditioner broke, I had to rush my daughter to the ER, the roof started leaking, my car stopped working. I ended up in the ER, and the effects of the virus would delay the reopening of schools and adjust the format of how schools would operate when they do open for the New Year 2020/2021. As a single parent, how would I homeschool my daughter when I needed to go back to work? With all of that said, it was also a sad time for my family as by October the fourth family member had died from COVID, and I knew of friends who either passed or recovered from COVID. To top it all off, this was also an election year with the weight of social justice or lack thereof as a pivotal point that would influence the outcome of the election. Once again, I went back to God, with all my whys, hows, and "what ifs."

I was broken, tired, exhausted, frustrated, and mentally drained. Have you ever felt like this? I cried out to God, and He gave me Miranda Curtis's "You Are My Strength." You see, praise and worship songs are what break me down, then lift me up, and take me back to God to stand before Him as He takes me down memory lane, again to remind me that He knows my need, He is all I need, and He's got me, and so it begins.

The online school year officially closed early in June, and my office reopened, with restrictions, in, June only taking back staff in the office on a need bases. I was again selected as one of those employees to return to the office. I asked God how I would manage during the summer months now that I needed to go back to work. How would I work out childcare as there were no summer programs? One day, while visiting Ms. Sally, an elderly woman I care for, a familiar visitor stopped by, we connected, and I learned that she is an educator who lost her job during COVID. She immediately said, "Look no further. I specialized in summer camps and projects for kids. I will help you for the summer." This was along with two other people God had placed in my path.

School was about to reopen; the public school system would be 100 percent online. When I contacted the school, I was told my daughters placed was one of the first to be secured because of early registration; look at God!

During the work-from-home COVID period, I was on reduced hours, which affected bill payments. I was not consistent with my tithe/offering. In August, after sewing my tithe to a worthy cause, two friends reached out in dire need, and without hesitation, I extended financial help to one and the other in kind. That same month in preparation for going back to school and having no bills paid yet, God doubled what I needed through two different sources to cover my overhead and back to school supplies in both cash and kind.

One Saturday in October while running errands on the road, I received an email late in the evening stating my daughter's school would be closed for fourteen days beginning on Monday as a teacher and her child tested positive for COVID. God already had a plan for this moment that He orchestrated two years prior. My aunt, who is usually working, would be off as of that Monday. God reminded me that He is an on time light in the darkness. My aunt was scheduled to go to Jamaica to attend the funeral of the last family member whose life was claimed by COVID, and this was her reason to be off that Monday. Everyone I reached out to was not available except one. Two years ago, I joined a support program at a local church and met Margaret, who has become a good friend. We later discovered many similarities between us. She was a working nurse at the time until she lost her job just before school opened and was still unemployed. While talking to her I mentioned the email from my daughter's school. She immediately said, "Petula, I'm not working. I will help you."

Prior to that week while visiting her at home for a special occasion, I met a mutual friend, a neighbor, who is a part of my alma mater and a kindergarten teacher. So, my daughter would not only be in a safe environment, but would also have access to a teacher's guide. My God, that is who You are!

Some say 2020 is a year of doom and gloom; some say it's an anomaly. I say it's the year of perfect vision. It's the year that God kept breaking me and molding me to see that He is my way maker and my light in the darkness. My faith in God has been tested, tried, and proven. But through it all, my big takeaway is to trust in Him because everything I have is a gift from God. Once I keep my eyes fixed on Him, not looking to the left or right. He will take care of me because He is 2020. He is perfect vision.

CHAPTER TWELVE:
CAN WE BREATHE?

SHARON PATTERSON-CAPEK

COVID Wars

Life framed within this existential crisis
I remember the pain like it was yesterday
My tears fall freely without a name
I remember people's guilt and a tint of shame
I remember the exhaustion of trying to explain

I remember the mothers look and their pain
Why are we so hard to see yet still get blamed
I remember 2020 because it was me
We trust in Christ for complete victory.

This is based on the harsh realities of racism that we face as people of color living in America. I was hit in the face with the truth after the murder of an American Black man named George Floyd. There were people who I thought I knew would speak up on the blatant injustice who were silent and remained silent. Then I heard their voices echoing, "He deserved it."

My heart was broken again. Covert racism has been embodied in our socio and economic culture, and we are still being asked questions while the truth is glaring. This was painful and still is. I grew up in Kingston, Jamaica, and the subject of race was never discussed in my family, elementary school, or high school. As a child, I was acutely aware of classicism and various stereo types within our culture. It was important to go to a certain elementary school, and the stress of passing the common entrance exam was every child's nightmare because our entire future depended upon it.

Fast-forward to my leaving the Caribbean and going to college in a large city. This city, though diverse racially and culturally, and while aspects of these cultures were celebrated, like the food and festivities, was not a sign that I would be "grandfathered in" based on the color of my skin. Someone said, "You speak so well." I thought he was referring to my

"You speak so well." I thought he was referring to my accent. Nope. He never thought that I would be fluid in the English language or have reasoning capabilities based on the color of my skin. When someone that I worked with asked me where I lived, and when I told them, they naturally assumed the worst part of town. Regardless of some of the obvious hate, it took a long time to get it. I did not grow up thinking about the color of my skin daily, and now, because of my experiences, I started questioning people's phrases, not sure if they were insulting me or it was just sheer insensitivity because it was covered. It was covert racism.

When the film *The Great Debaters* was released, that was the turning point. The film was based on life in America in the 1940s and starred Forest Whitaker. He and his family were traveling in their car down a country road when he hit a large hog. The terror on their faces was imminent, and what this implied was nauseating. It was payday and a celebration for their family because of dreams that would be fulfilled. Two white males armed with their rifles approached him and demanded payment for the dead animal. He was forced to sign over his paycheck, and they also kept their three-hundred-pound pig. It was in that moment that I got it. I finally understood. It also occurred to me what life was like for people of color in a period when they had no rights. It became noticeably clearer with the impact of the price paid during the civil rights movement and after.

Because of the bravery of many men and women of color, I was given an opportunity. I wept for a very long time.

The death of George Floyd was heinous. He uttered, "I can't breathe," as a policeman knelt on his neck, cutting off the flow of oxygen for some eight minutes in view of other cops and onlookers. His death and the protests were not an isolated event. It became the culmination of the thousands of deaths at the hands of people who have said, "You have no right to be here."

I think a lot of us had a glimmer of expectation that something would change. The world was outraged by this; what was America going to do? Surely a change has come. To say I was appalled by the responses or the lack thereof from people that I thought I knew and those whom I didn't was an understatement. In various chats on social media, the narrative was consistent with the thousands who died before him: "He was high." He was a derelict. He was a something or other.

I asked numerous times to appeal to reasonable doubt. I asked if it were OK for someone to be murdered because they did wrong and if grace existed for a man who, from what I understood, had turned his life around. When a crime is committed, why are people of color never assigned the narrative of being mentally ill when this has protected a select few in various confrontations with blue? I was not expecting the racist rhetoric in support of murder from church folk. I realized in that moment we were at a great divide, an impasse. All lives cannot matter until Black lives do. We cannot remain invisible while others engage in cultural misappropriations.

The 2020 pandemic has taken a lot of lives; it has been a tragedy, and our hearts grieve with those who have lost their loved ones. Even though this is unequivocally one of the worse periods in this century, we have been graced with time, time to live differently, to see what was already in front of us, and to move away from relationships that have been caustic, to embrace the relationship of a loving Heavenly Father who is waiting to love us, to get a career and not a job, to see the beauty around us despite the pain, to be intentional with our generosity, to receive love, and finally to breathe.

CHAPTER THIRTEEN:

REFLECTIONS OF ONE'S DIVINE PURPOSE

MEGAN AND PRINCE ADERELE

One of the things we believe as a couple is that everyone is Divine. That said:

Dear Divine One, we greet you with the master word: Shalom.

The global pandemic of 2020 propelled individuals from all walks of life to tap into their potential to define their purpose and prosperity. There was a heightened level of spiritual awareness that just did not seem to exist before. If there is one thing that this pandemic taught career seekers and business owners, it is that if it is your calling, then it will keep calling you. Ultimately, everyone has two choices: answer it or continue to do nothing.

The year 2020 also gave people the audacity to unapologetically walk in their divine purpose by truly getting still enough to learn how to connect deeper to the God of their faith. It was like everyone was going through a spiritual awakening of some sort based upon their beliefs, faith, practices, and experiences. During this pandemic, when some considered this to be a period of quarantine, it became a healing retreat for many others. We often want resolutions, but healing must first come from within. This period of healing and growth provided the opportunity to gain clarity of vision and purpose.

Businesses were birthed during this season, which for one reason or another caused many to break free from the traditional 9–5, where they found time to work within their passion and higher calling. Not everyone has a desire to become an entrepreneur; however, most will not argue the fact that most everyone has a desire to make additional money.

Whatever your money mission is, the key is to align it to your higher purpose. **We became clear on our collective mission, as The Aditú Agency.**

As both of us are the children of ministers, we knew that our life's mission would involve being of service to others as it was instilled to each of us at birth. As business owners, 2020 became our year that propelled a greater mission to empower others to tap into their spirituality so that they can walk in their divine purpose and personal power. Growing up, we both saw many powerful and talented struggling "spiritual entrepreneurs" and wanted to empower others to create and accumulate their own wealth. So, remember, as you are on your own individual journey, tap into your divinity as a source of your creativity. You are a creator and have the ability to manifest.

We want to encourage you to get those ideas out of your mind and onto paper. You have to create that action plan and then commit to get started even before you feel ready. It's not every day that you hear of two individuals from two different continents whose families have been practicing spirituality for generations, but we're here, together, and 2020 solidified our life commitment to be of service to others.

Life for us on the outside looking in seemed perfect, but people are oblivious to the struggles. You see, it is the stories that people do not know or hear that truly shape one's drive, hustle, determination, and character.

Prince's Personal Reflection

Born into a Nigerian royal family with a veil over my eyes, which has been known as an indication of intuitiveness and spiritual endowment, I became a carrier of the intangible cultural heritage of my Yoruba ancestors at a young age. I decided to leave and choose my own path where no one knew me, so I embarked to the US under an arts and culture initiative.

Even after my leaving the only country that I knew and all of my immediate family, I noticed that the lockdown was also one of the loneliest times of my life from a business standpoint because I was used to attending in-person business and networking events. My wife always enjoyed being at home, so she transitioned into this time period much better than I, but after a while, it even got to her. This time highlighted the universal need for social interaction even if it were as small as a few words exchanged with people over video. We often stated that we were social distancing, but the correct term should have been "physical distancing," which was super important to those of us who were trying to keep our families well. It gave people a newfound appreciation for face-to-face interactions with family and friends.

With 1.7 million of lives lost to the pandemic, it made me rethink my priorities and remember how precious life truly is. It was a constant reminder to appreciate the small things in life, the things I often take for granted such as friends and family. With so many deaths each day, I quickly became grateful for my family and friends even if it meant video calls and text messages when we could not see each other in person. With so many people falling ill, I was grateful mostly for my health, my marriage, my kids, and my ability to have multiple sources of income. It saddened me that many other talented people were struggling and could not find ways to reinvent themselves.

This pandemic made me reevaluate my life and assess my priorities and has served as a reminder of how precious life is and to always appreciate the small things. My wish for you is for you to always do the same. Celebrate life each day. Adúpé *(Thank you in Yoruba)*

Megan's Personal Reflection

I grew up in a nondenominational Christian temple my grandmother started in 1942. My father oversaw the church until his death. While I was growing up, my family also had a candle shop run by my aunt. I always knew that we were more spiritual than religious, both because my friends always said that my family was different and because when I visited other churches, I saw how closed-minded, unaccepting, and judgmental many were. I was taught to respect all and to find the value in the lessons from other religious texts and spiritual practices. You see, I never thought deeply about what to call my family because I thought it was the norm. I grew up learning about meditation, astrology, numerology, prayer, affirmations, burning candles, other forms of energy, and that when we worship, we do so in spirit and in truth.

At the tender age of twelve, I unexpectedly lost both parents. Technically orphaned, I was raised by two older sisters and a brother. But at this pivotal time in my life, not only did I lose my parents and foundational spiritual teachers, but I also lost distant siblings, aunts, uncles, and other family who never fostered their relationship with me. Despite this tragedy, I still did what I had to do. I went to college, got advanced degrees, and got a "good job." The instability early on in my life from the loss of my parents to being degreed and laid off three times propelled me to seek my purpose.

As the world around me and others began to shut down, I first learned the importance of forgiveness to healing. Oftentimes, we look to others for acceptance and healing. But we have to heal from within. We have to first forgive ourselves for the things that we know and the things that we do not know so that we can truly forgive other people. I finally accepted the fact that I am a healer, and I now know that I come from generations of metaphysical teachers and healers.

Growing up, when people had problems, I helped them figure out a solution. I was always full of ideas and saw that solutions came to me naturally, so I found a career in business and education. For years, I was a business strategist and career coach who just so happened to talk about spirituality with her clients. I always felt like a Jack (well, Jill) of all trades and master of none. This pandemic allowed me to own the fact that all of my combined experiences and background shaped the spiritual and business gifts that I have to offer. I had to go through more than most to be able to relate to and help to empower others.

My time in solitude allowed me to connect not just with my kids but also with myself. I am more spiritual than I am business-oriented and totally operate in that zone of genius and have no shame to let people know that spirituality has played a pivotal role in my life and in my business. This year encouraged me to take on my family's mantle by undeniably walking in my God-given purpose. We as divine beings all have the ability to act as channels and should strive to use our gifts to empower others. I encourage you to do the same.

Life and Legacy Lessons: **A Soul Work Self-reflection Exercise**

One's soul purpose and personal power can be confusing topics. Many people question their purpose, or more specifically they pose a question to themselves such as, "God, why me?" Too many people are pretending that they're not spiritually gifted and need to stop pretending that they're not operating with the spirit. What truths/facts have you been omitting? Who are you, really?

A spiritual shift happens when you lose the self that you know for your truest self. Your gifts are not free, and you must accept the fact that you're the master of your divinity and spirituality. Define your growth and purpose plan.

Everything that you want is already chasing you so you must ask yourself what you need. What do you want? Who do you want with you on this journey? Remember, the key to everything is to be of service. How will you be of service to others?

Having a religious connection is different from having a spiritual connection, and this pandemic pushed people to connect to the God of their faith through prayer (speaking to God) and meditation (allowing God to speak to you). How do you understand when God speaks to you?

Remember, It Starts with You

No one is coming to save you. You have to save yourself, but to do so, you must heal yourself first, which means that you have to seek first to understand and then to be understood. You have to focus on your own spiritual journey: your growth, your healing, your grace, your forgiveness, your faith, your health, and your circle.

You must take an inventory of your life and do the things that truly matter. You have to learn how to manifest your dreams and goals by leveraging your gifts and superpowers. You have to strengthen your strengths and be inspired to continuously heal yourself, which means that everyone should not have access to you, so starting from today always commit to protecting your energy. Action is faith in yourself. Remember, it starts with you.

This global pandemic allowed us to reevaluate our entire business model, messaging, and marketing. Instead of just talking about spirituality with our clients, we birthed a new vision that allowed us both to fully operate in our gifts, our calling, and our purpose, collectively and individually. We became unmasked to stop hiding in our business and truly embody that our earthly assignment was to be the spiritual mentors that we never had.

We can see that 2020 was a year of growth, expansion, adaptability, and achievements. Whichever year you read this, Divine One, know that, this is your year. It starts with you. It starts now!

We pray for your continued success as well as love and light on your path to greatness. And so, it is. Asé.

CHAPTER FOURTEEN:
CALLED TO SERVE DESPITE ADVERSITY

NICOLE SMALL-FLETCHER

If you've read the last thirteen chapters, you know that the year 2020 was synonymous with the coronavirus pandemic that changed the world and people's lives. My life too changed right here in Florida when I received the phone call from my sister, Khristen, about our mother, Jennifer's, health. Mom was experiencing excruciating pain in her right big toe in February

2020 because of issues with diabetes. When Khristen took her to the hospital in March 2020, the doctors did not know what to do. In the meantime, coronavirus had increased across the world, and people were dying. My life has been hectic for the last couple of years with my husband's diagnosis of colon cancer, children, building the business, school, and ministry.

I decided I had to go to my mother. I began traveling every week for a three- hour drive back and forth between our homes. It hurt to see the vibrant Jennifer unable to do the things that she loved. She worried about her independence. Independence is freedom from the control, influence, support, aid, and the like of others. Khristen experienced fear and doubt about Mom's health and being able to help her. During this pandemic, I have seen people being affected by being dependent upon a job, doctors, government, the system, and people for everyday essentials for their family and home. It is a system that seems to be against the livelihood of people. The pandemic for society has become either having the coronavirus, losing your independence to others, or knowing God has got you.

I instantly became a caregiver for her medical decisions and appointments, a dietitian, and an intercessor walking by faith for healing. I was making decisions I never had to make before for another person. The doctors said she has gangrene in her toe due to low blood circulation from diabetes. The doctors suggested amputation, and she said no. I have never seen anyone experience the pain that my mother experienced.

Every prescription drug could not ease or stop the pain. We had many sleepless nights. When I prayed for her, the pain would stop, and she was able to sleep. I changed her entire diet and mindset toward food. She developed a dependence on the doctors and medications that gripped her life. The pain intensified, and the gangrene spread to the second toe. I knew God was not done with her yet. Her experience was more significant than mine, so I became a light in her life to make a difference. I put everything aside and learned compassion, patience, kindness, gentleness, faithfulness, self-control, perseverance, listening, and how to meet her needs.

I began to pray differently because this was a situation where amputation in my mother's mind meant losing her independence. Errol and I came into agreement that Jehovah Rapha was his healer as the righteousness of God created in Christ Jesus with power and authority. Together, we learned we must have faith in the Word of God, in God's willingness and ability to perform His Word on our behalf, and have faith to decree and declare God's Word." I shared my testimony with Mom about how God healed my husband Errol from stage-4 colon cancer. I prayed with her and led her to Jesus Christ for salvation. I read the Word of God, studied the Word of God, and prayed the Word of God over her life. Daily I declared the Word of God by faith over my mother's body to be transformed, have regular blood sugar, and heal. I witnessed normal blood sugar levels and the cleansing of her body. I believed that God could transform and heal her. Jesus referred to the power of the Holy Spirit in John 3:34 *that is available to everyone.* God clothed me with the power of the Holy Spirit because I cannot do anything apart from His Spirit. God provided the stamina I needed to complete the work in my mother's life. I have seen excellent blood sugar levels, and the doctors decreased her medications. I had to remember that God has a will and way for my mother, and I had to come to grasp that reality because she depended on me to fix it.

In September 2020, Mom and Khristen moved to the city I reside in three hours away because we were not pleased with the doctors. We went to see a new doctor. Jennifer was crying because of the pain, she said to their doctor, "I have had this pain since March. I cannot do it anymore. I am tired. If you cannot stop the pain, then amputate." My mouth fell open because I did not expect it, but I knew I was called to serve her through this experience. Jesus called us to be a servant of all because we serve God by meeting the temporal and spiritual needs of those around us. Helping others is a tool the Lord uses to free us of selfishness by lowering us to a servant level. God called me to serve my mother and sister, and I truly understood what it meant to know how to make a difference in their lives. On October 22, they amputated her right leg below the knee and she did not even cry. The first five days were tough because of the phantom pain. She told me that the foot was still there along with the pain, and it feels weird.

The pain subsided quickly. The hospital moved her to rehabilitation after five days, and she excelled in aggressive physical therapy. She remained positive, completed physical therapy, and was fitted with a prosthetic leg. Getting her independence back is what drove her to keep going. Jennifer went home on November 9 and is in physical therapy at home. I have become her strength when she is depressed about losing her independence because she feels she is now a burden. My mother's persistence is remarkable because it has outweighed her depression. God has been my rock throughout these months of seeing her in pain and now as an amputee. Jennifer still has some more weeks ahead of her to get back her independence.

I have experienced a lot of adversity, which is a condition marked by misfortune, calamity, or distress. I have overcome adversity once again because God is my strength. During these times, we cannot give up. We must remember our why. I have been so busy caring about my mother, sister, husband, marriage, business, and ministry that I forgot there was a pandemic because God has provided, protected, and expanded our territory. We have not been affected by the virus because we have placed our faith in Jesus Christ to keep us. God has given me a great responsibility to accomplish His work here on earth. Every person I have encountered I am determined to meet them where they are now and meet their needs. As a woman of God, I am clothed with power, called to serve, and must make a difference to others through Jesus Christ in this world.

CHAPTER FIFTEEN:

2020 THE YEAR OF HUMBLING

GRACE ANN LONG

Looking back on January 1, 2020 to now, I see so much has changed in my life and around me. I have seen a lot of divorces and a lot more families separated because they were forced to be in their homes with their significant other rather than on the road. Companies have been shut down after years of being open.

The year 2020 has taught me the importance of faith and prayer. But through it all, I can say, "Thank you, Lord, for all the experiences of this past year and the times of success that will always be happy memories with my home and personal walk with You." The scripture says, "For whosoever exalteth himself shall be abased; and he that humbles himself shall be exalted." In 2020, God humbled most of us. COVID has been a rough period: so many people lost their lives, so many got sick, and so many lost jobs, homes, food, and shelter.

The times of failure reminded me of my own weakness and of my need for God. With the physical building of the church being closed, it showed many that churches are not the physical building that they worship, but, in fact, the church is us. It has taught me the true meaning of ministry and helping people is about how we help people and how we treat people in general. Would we let the homeless bathe in our church? Would we let them sit on the nice clean bench? We all are so happy dressing in our Sunday's best that we often forgot that God would use the people that other people don't count.

When you go through a problem in life, or better yet a crisis, you approach God differently. Think about it. You pray and worship from your belly's bottom. Your worship is different because you need something from your Father. To grow in any area, you must be tested, and it is when you lose control when you know that God is in control. When God sends a storm, He knows why he sends it. God showed us that man is just human, and every system can crash but His system. Even with the physical doors being closed, I have never seen so many people worshiping and praying in history. People who have never cried out to God cried out. Yes, we lost love ones; yes, we lost money, jobs, and everything that money can buy.

Nevertheless, He shows us that the act of kindness and salvation is free. Living in grace isn't easy, but grace allows you to live daily. The greatest things happen through the hardest times of anyone's life. I am still thanking God because He is God.

I remember hearing someone say, "He had to break your heart to save your life." What we call wisdom God calls foolishness. He does not need help. Doctors and scientists realized that they had to rely more on God than their gifts. I saw nurses and doctors praying inside hospitals. God made His presence known to me that His kingdom is not about earning and deserving. It is about believing and receiving. I can say that I may not have experienced some of the worst, but God has blessed me during this COVID. Not to say I don't feel other's pain. However, "Blessing of the Lord makes rich and adds no sorrow."

It took us having to kneel to God. It took lives for a way to find a better way of doing things. It took COVID for most of us to appreciate the simple things. We didn't need to be impeccably dressed all the time or overspend on things we cannot afford. We went nowhere but the grocery store. It took COVID for some of us to treat our bodies as temples. It took COVID for some to eat right, act right, and simply be right. Through it all, I have learned that the blessing is in the process, and even though we are still processing, I do believe that I can only lean on my faith and trust in God not just in good times but in bad. COVID taught me that the biggest blessing or the most important blessing I could receive is air. You can be blind and still live, but I do not know anyone who doesn't have air who is walking around. I thank God for His grace. He allowed us to live through it.

CHAPTER SIXTEEN:

HEAVEN'S P.P.P. (PREPARATION FOR PROGRESS IN A PANDEMIC)

LAWANDA C. HARRIS

If 2020 taught us anything, it's just how important it is for us to be mentally, spiritually, and physically prepared to navigate major changes in our lives. We have been taught the importance of being grounded enough to plan, flexible enough to pivot, and fortified to win during challenging times. While this pandemic seems to have blindsided many, there may be a pattern to note that helps us prepare before the next pandemic strikes.

A business colleague mentioned to me that every ten years, there is a global disruption that alters the way we live, work, and conduct business. At the time, I did not give it much thought until I discovered that pattern within my own experiences, navigating three global disruptions during my adulthood. These disruptions were distant enough to not seem connected but close enough to suggest a pattern when I looked a little closer. There was Y2K in 1999, the financial crisis and housing market crash of 2008 that spilled over into 2009, and now COVID-19 that held the entire year of 2020 tightly in its grip.

Whether the arrival of these global events form a pattern or are purely coincidental is for the conspiracy theorists and nightly news pundits to hash out. I just know that in all three, I fared exceptionally well because of the season of preparation that organically occurred right before each of these global events that I have named "Heaven's P. P. P."

In 1999, when Y2K was all the rage, we were just getting comfortable with how technology was changing our everyday lives. According to a History.com 2019 article, the World Wide Web did not become publicly recognizable until nine years earlier, in 1990. There was still a lot we did not know about the machines that would soon run our entire lives. For those of us around at the turn of the new century, there was global anxiety about what was going to happen when 1999 rolled into 2000. No one really knew what to expect, and there was plenty of subjective speculation.

There were outrageous rumors that the earth could fall off its axis and a religious sect who predicted it was going to be the end of the world. All the doom and gloom talk flooded the airwaves and seemingly inspired Prince to create a song about partying like it was our last day on earth. Do you remember? Y2K left quite a mark!

Nearly a decade later, a financial crisis reminiscent of the Great Depression hit the global economy in October 2008 and wreaked havoc throughout 2009. Corporate greed and risky mortgage lending practices within the banking industry sent the economy into a tailspin.

The stock market plummeted nearly 777 points in one day. Major corporations that appeared recession-proof, like Lehman Brothers and Washington Mutual, filed for bankruptcy. Companies closed, millions lost their jobs, retirement accounts, homes, credit, and financial security overnight. The crisis was so bad, that the entire banking industry required a bailout from the U.S. Government.

Hindsight being 20/20 (no pun intended), it appears my colleague may have been right. There does seem to be a pattern of global disruptions spaced approximately ten years apart. I just did not make the connection until COVID-19 hit the scene, and here is how it came together.

In 2017, I found out I was getting a divorce from my third husband seventy-seven days after returning from our annual anniversary vacation. It was totally unexpected. We were not having any disagreements or fighting. We were a loving couple whom many people admired.

The full story of the decline of my marriage is for another book, but the takeaway is that I was completely arrested by a pain that overwhelmed my existence. I cried for months and fell into a deep, dark, lonely road of depression. I was inconsolable. The rejection was palpable. You could see it on my countenance. I cried myself to sleep every night and could barely get out of bed many days.

My ex-husband weighed over 300 pounds physically, but the trauma I carried weighed even more. And that is many of our realities when it comes to trauma. We miss opportunities because we get weighed down with the baggage of our past. Soul singer Erykah Badu sang about it in her year 2000 hit single, "Bag Lady:"

Bag lady you gone hurt your back
Dragging all them bags like that
I guess nobody ever told you
All you must hold onto, is you
One day all them bags gon' get in your way,
So, pack light

I was the bag lady.

My divorce was finalized on November 28, 2018 after twenty-two months of agony (twenty of which was spent estranged under the same roof). I carried that trauma throughout 2019 and began 2020, still crying, still talking about it, and still missing my estranged husband every day. I was paralyzed within myself, war-torn by the pain, and basically broken to my core.

Fast-forward to February 8, 2020. I had an overwhelmingly strong desire to attend a worship experience, called **Lovestruck**™ which manifests verifiable miracles every year. I mentioned that desire in a circle of friends after a homegoing celebration earlier that day. One of my friends with firsthand knowledge of the event discouraged me from going, citing the event had over-committed the complimentary tickets, and I would never get inside. As I left that fellowship, I decided to tune into the service on my phone as I drove home. The energy in the room could be felt through the airwaves. People were rejoicing, and the atmosphere was ripe for captives to be set free. From the initial looks, it appeared my friend was right. It was standing room only. Suddenly, one camera operator accidentally showed a whole section of empty seats in the balcony. I immediately made a legal U-turn and drove to the location to participate in the remainder of the service.

I arrived just before the intermission and discreetly sat in the back where the lights were low, and no one knew me. As I sat in that atmosphere, I began to weep. I cried out to God from the depths of my soul. I told Him how much I wanted to be free from the bondage of living in the shadow of my ex-husband, who had broken my heart into pieces and seemingly just moved on with his life. I sat in the back of that auditorium and allowed God to peel layer after layer of hurt, pain, disruption, anger, lack of forgiveness, defeat, and rejection off my life. By the time that night was over, I could physically feel the weight of that burden lift off my life. I was free to march forth into my next level of greatness without carrying that excessive weight. It was not until then that I could see myself healed, whole, and healthy.

Immediately, I was able to start living again versus merely just existing. I started working on creative projects, building new business concepts, and was making upward progress when in true-to-form fashion, COVID-19 entered the scene and brought the world to its knees. There does seem to be a pattern to these major catastrophic events that alter the trajectory of how we live every ten years.

But when I evaluated my personal experiences, there seemed to be a period of strategic preparation to help us progress. Consider my experiences:

- In 1999, approximately ten months before Y2K fever hit, I was gifted a brand-new computer system with up-to-date software through a program my son was enrolled in. The calendar turned over perfectly fine, and all my files entered the new millennium with me fully intact.

- In 2008, I completed a full audit of my financial health and repaired any issues on my credit report. This put me in position to purchase my first home for a third of what it would have otherwise cost, in a highly desirable market, during the worst economic downturn since the Great Depression.

- In 2020, my heart was healed just one month before COVID-19 hit, which helped me get unstuck. This afforded me the opportunity to relaunch one of my corporate brands and land two national blue-chip clients when millions of people were losing their jobs. This is Heaven's P.P.P., not to be confused with the U.S. Government's P.P.P. (Paycheck Protection

Program), where small businesses were able to take out government loans to stay afloat during the 2020 pandemic. Heaven's P.P.P. is far more valuable in equipping the saints for the work ahead (Ephesians 4:12), pulling down strongholds

(2 Corinthians 10:3), and setting captives free (Luke 4:18).

For me, Heaven's P.P.P., proved far more lucrative. It helped me lay aside the baggage I carried that essentially had me in a state of paralysis. Heaven's P.P.P. downloads fresh, new, and creative ideas. It illuminates pathways and orders our footsteps so we can boldly proclaim the "Lords' doing, which is marvelous in our eyes" (Psalms 118:23).

Through my own experiences and hearing the stories of countless others who have fared exceptionally well during this pandemic, I am fully persuaded that if something catastrophic happens every ten years, God is always a few steps ahead and has made a way for us to escape.

Our Advocate will not sleep or slumber. He will see to it that we always come out on top. Believe me when I tell you nothing can stop your God or your genius. Embrace that today. The plans He has for you are unstoppable because He takes care of His own. I am a witness. Heaven prepares us to progress during a pandemic.

Today, I am a healed, healthy, and vibrant woman who is heavily pursuing every God given gift, talent, and ability I possess. I am convinced that what I went through in this last season has the power to help others. If you need support overcoming the challenges of heartbreak after divorce, this story was written just for you. I invite you to join my online community at facebook. com/chroniclespda where we are helping people understand their history so they can live well in the present.

CHAPTER SEVENTEEN:
I WAS NOT READY FOR THE FINAL CHAPTER

QUE JOHNSON

I have to be honest; 2019 did not prepare me for 2020. The two things I didn't plan to do in a million years were to write a final chapter (farewell) for one of my favorite people in the universe and becoming an author. But I have thirty reasons to share what 2020 taught me, brought me, and took away from me. I also have thirty reasons why I refused to let the negative of the year break me.

Question: Have you ever felt a weight so heavy on your heart you couldn't speak? Well, that was me all 2020; you will discover this to be true in my writing as well. I'm sure you will feel the hurt, pain, and the healing as well. I was raised in a modest-sized family, and through all the good and bad times we were always taught to love each other and be there no matter what. My mother was birthed from an extraordinarily strong woman, my grandmother Katherine Johnson, who transitioned in 1997. Our immediate family has been very blessed over the past two decades to be survived by my grandmother. Most of us are fortunate enough to know very well a grandmother's love, and she adored her sixteen grandchildren—not to take away from the rest of the family, but the bond was different. Growing up, we always came together to support each other's accomplishments, birthdays, holidays, and the usual "just because it's Tuesday" tradition.

There was a bond between us first cousins that felt more like we're all siblings, and because we vary in age, some are closer than others. This was all we knew for the past twenty-three years since 1997, but that shattered in 2020 in the midst of a pandemic, and instead of celebrating a joyous occasion, we found ourselves in devastation. One of Katherine Johnson's sixteen grandchildren has taken a hit; actually, he took thirty hits. The cousin I was closest to, more like my little brother, my protector, was taken away from me. It still feels like yesterday when I received the dreaded phone call. I play it over and over in my head, and I recall hearing, "He's dead; He's dead," I screamed so hard I remember the phone falling. In that moment I felt nothing below my waist as I fell to the floor.

Once our family was notified and preparations were being made, my mother volunteered me to write his obituary. How would I find the strength? This is the final chapter. We're in the middle of a pandemic and funerals have become challenging because of our new normal called social distancing, prohibited contact, and mask wearing. What would this mean for the elders and other family members who need to travel in town to pay their last respects? Filled with many concerns, I took on the challenge, and with every pen stroke, I felt the pain of reality, anger, and hurt sinking in. I couldn't comprehend the words I was writing, I had to speak for those whom he was leaving behind, what he was like, and what we will miss about him. As my family continued to make final arrangements I was wishing this were all a bad dream that I would wake up from. Unfortunately, it wasn't as the time came to say goodbye.

As I looked around me and the world, time was still moving. I knew in that moment I had to lean on and press into God like I never did before. At times it's so hard to look at my aunt or even speak with her on the phone knowing her only son is no longer with us, but I continue to lean on God. It also made me love my sons in a different way, as I'm getting a better understanding of God's love. My cousin's passing taught me to work my passion harder because I wasn't living up to my fullest potential and my goals weren't big enough. Since then, I have made a special goal. I plan to make a million dollars for every bullet that entered my precious cousin's body. He was shot thirty times, so yes, that's 30 million in my business, 529 Management. You can check us out. Although I suffered a family loss, my business saw some great wins. I refuse to lose because I know a believer can never be defeated.

And just when I thought I had learned all the lessons I could learn from 2020, as I close this chapter, I got the news that my mother was admitted to the hospital with COVID-19. She's now on a ventilator that will breathe for her. I know it is one pandemic, but it sure feels like it is a legion of pandemics with one piece of one bad news after another. Can you relate? My heart aches again. My boys are asking for Grandma. It's near Christmas; we were supposed to have a great Christmas, I cannot tell you how many times I have asked, "Why Lord?"

Though I wasn't ready to write the final chapter, God thought I was ready to hold the pen. I have placed my faith in Him to do the impossible and unexplainable so that those who doubt Him can behold His goodness. There are no such things as little missions when you are created for big results.

CHAPTER EIGHTEEN:

THE GENESIS

DR. PUNITHA RATHNAM

It was raining when she left, a gentle drizzle, nothing like the storm raging in her heart.

She did not know at the time that it was a new beginning.

She just knew that her life couldn't stay the same.

The sky had been clear, and she could see the stars through the window above the long driveway and a gravel road ahead. She remembered the first time she had come to this house as a young bride, frightened and far away from home. This house had come to represent all that she despised.

A golden cage is still a cage, and a bird longs to soar the skies when for so many years her wings were clipped.

Like many Indian women of her generation, she married her parents' choice. She would never have chosen him, even though by most standards he was considered handsome and accomplished, an Indian mother-in-law's dream. She preferred gentleness, and looks were a poor substitute for a kind voice and integrity.

She had never imagined love or, in her wildest thoughts, romance. She would have settled for acceptance, maybe even respect with two souls on the same journey. But what unfolded was demeaning, making her feel less than human.

The relationship, never good; even at first, it was like a blow.

The arguments were acrimonious and the abuse insidious; only sometimes physical, usually a barrage of words, manipulation, and fear.

Being married to a bully is a constant attrition of self-esteem, like living in a home with a dripping faucet of never-ending innuendo, and contempt.

She barely recognized the woman who stared back at her from the mirror. She used to be happy, self-confident, and proud of her achievements; now she was a shell. The years had robbed her of so much.

This night would change her life forever in ways she could never imagine. As she walked down the dark driveway, her thoughts were not to the future, only on trying to escape a dangerous present.

The future was uncertain; what she was certain about was that God was on her side, despite what she was forced to hide. A pandemic failed in comparison to what she carried.

CHAPTER NINETEEN:
COVID CHRONICLES

SONIA WHITE

I was fired from my job in November right before the holidays in 2019. It was the most devastating time of my life, not only because of the holidays. I had little to no savings and had been struggling for some years. I was hired at a local travel agency in Houston and did a few jobs here and there just barely making my bills. I had my twin sons Dakari and Demetrius in college. I went through tremendous depression.

In January 2020, an opportunity came up for me to take a travel job in Browning, Montana on an Indian reservation of the Blackfeet tribe. I was reluctant because I heard how cold it was, and I was not one for cold weather or below-freezing temperatures. I was sold on the perks, and it was only for thirteen weeks, and if I did not like it, could return to Houston with my flight paid. It also would be an opportunity to have a regular paycheck coming in. I arrived in January, and it was 0 degrees, and to my shock the temperatures reached -26 degrees; you read that right: negative 26 degrees. I was near Cutbank, Montana, which is documented as the coldest place in the United States where it reached a record-breaking -47 degrees in 1936. I had to look twice to see if this temperature were a mistake on the bank's billboard.

This was pre-COVID, so everything was fine, and I was getting acclimated to driving in the snow, fierce high winds, and freezing weather. There was news about the China outbreak that occurred in December 2019 and a virus that I really did not pay attention to since it did not affect the US. Everything became worrisome in February and from then on. It was a challenging time because I was scheduled to see my son run track, and everything was canceled. I had not seen my twin boys in college for over a year since they lived in Los Angeles. When the snow began to melt at the end of April and May, I was able to visit Glacier National Park, which is less than an hour's drive away from the Blackfeet Indian

Reservation. This is when I fell in love with Montana. Glacier Park is definitely God's country, and the air was so pure and fresh; the lakes were the color of turquoise as if they had been pained; the mountains were topped with snow, and the waterfalls were like images on a postcard. The beauty was breathless, and I also learned it is bear country so I learned a lot about bear safety and precautions in addition to other wildlife. I had never seen such as moose, mountain goats, elk, mountain lions, wolves, and beavers: things I read about in books but never saw in real life.

The COVID cases began to increase dramatically after a funeral on the reservation some locals attended. The implication was, however, not certain. The cases at the hospital spiked dramatically, and, fortunately, we are at a government hospital that had sufficient supplies of PPE. It took a toll on me and fellow staff because we were praying that we took all the precautions and prayed that we would not contract the virus with every other patient testing COVID positive.

The COVID crisis did impact a lot of people with job loss and so many deaths in 2020. I was fortunate to have a job and felt like God set me up personally prior to COVID for a great opportunity that has allowed me to invest in myself, and it was the first time in my life I was isolated and able to focus on me; my relationship with God went to a next level, and He became my best friend and showed me in a time of crisis when I did not have one person to really call or vent to that He had me. I set up a prayer table and began a journey of reading since I did not have a television for nine months on my travel assignment, and it was one of the most productive times in my entire life. I invested in audio books and hard-copy books and began reading my Bible, which provided tremendous comfort. I also began journaling and making it a routine to speak to God regularly.

One of the most enlightening experiences during COVID was the presidential election of Joe Biden, Jr., and Vice President Kamala Harris. Being from Texas, I did a mail-in ballot for the first time in my life. I was proud, and my adult children also voted. It was a family affair. This election was incredibly stressful since we had to wait a few days for the results. I was on edge, and although we have a Black female as vice president, this is no reason to be lackadaisical or complacent.

We must work harder than ever before; nothing will be given to us in life no matter who is in office. It is refreshing to see what the future holds for the country and this new leadership. It has been an interesting journey working during COVID on the Indian reservation. Cases began increasing, and nearly one out of three patients were COVID-positive. We followed strict personal protective equipment protocols when doing procedures on patients. I would like to say that this experience has been enlightening and sparked my inner entrepreneur spirit in writing books as I have always wanted to do, completing my degree, and a lot of reading. It also allowed me to focus on my time with God and build the relationship with Him and my scheduled one-on-one time. It made me appreciate life even more, and what really mattered was time spent with family, staying healthy, and pursuing my dreams and aspirations with no regrets. I felt like a cocooned and soon-to-bloom butterfly with all that I have experienced with COVID. It was also an eye opener because a lot of people I expected to be there for me even in conversation and support were not. God showed me that ultimately, He was the only One I could rely on and that at the end of the day it is a relationship with Him that mattered. This period gave me strength and courage that I did not know I had, and I found that being alone did not mean being lonely. My dating was null and void, and this allowed me to grow and find happiness within myself.

I was never alone, my mom Gwendolyn, my daughter Maya, the twins and my best friend since the 2nd grade, Dr. Nicole Evans-Ross who kept me well informed and protected were there for me. Dr. Nicole is an Internist, she kept me up to date with important COVID-19 safety protocols that were often overlooked like, cleaning our cellphones and not sharing them with anyone or cleaning them thoroughly after sharing and frequently. Here are six other important COVID-19 safety and protection tips, these were from the CDC:

1. Wash hands often and frequently

2. Avoid close contact with others keep six feet distance

3. Cover mouth and nose with mask when around others

4. Cover cough and sneezes

5. Clean and disinfect regularly

6. Monitor your health daily and see a physician if you develop a fever or any other abnormal symptoms for early detection and treatment.

As I write this, a vaccine is being created by Pfizer and other pharmaceutical companies which will be available to the public and front line hospital workers as early as December 2020. So, by the time you read this, there 'may' be a cure. This has been an exhausting and trying year for health care workers, housekeeping staff, and the like, working long hours short-handed. Some states have nurses and doctors and allied health staff working who are COVID-positive as long as they are asymptomatic with the shortage of health care staffing. One quote I would like to leave here is, "Cherish every day; tomorrow is not promised to anyone, and live, love, and laugh frequently."

I made tremendous strides during the global pandemic. I started a nonprofit for young minority men, the S.M.I.L.E. Foundation (Smart Men in Leadership Excellence), to educate, encourage, and inspire young men to be successful in life and to reduce deaths among minority men from excessive law enforcement and hate crimes. Our website is www.smilementor.org. I was inspired by this several years ago, by the brutal death of Trayvon Martin, and others and now George Floyd, Breonna Taylor, and Ahmaud Arberry during the pandemic, and so many others who have lost their lives. My desire is to help save Black boys and men from future marginalization. Our website is www.smilementor.org

As I did community work with Black males, I began to feel tired. COVID fatigue is real, and it takes a toll on the body. Self-care is vital for front line workers and medical personnel. The housekeeping staff at the job did a wonderful job with our terminal cleanings required after every COVID-positive patient. Self-care suggestions include massage, enjoying nature and fresh air, being home alone mask free, music, completing a project, writing, painting, prayer and meditation, exercise of some form, yoga, talking to friends and loved ones who offer positive vibes and engaging conversations, and completing projects and a enjoying sense of accomplishment such as organizing your closet, garage, purging, and making a list of things you need to do. Make mini-goals to accomplish the larger goals and tasks. Some of the emotions I have experienced working directly with COVID-positive patients are fear, anxiety, grief, and gratitude.

I especially fear that I may contract the virus and spread it to my children and family. I feel anxiety because it has been overwhelming and working short-staffed, grief because coworkers became ill and some have lost their lives, and gratitude because God has given me the strength and the position to help others during this crisis and to have the stamina to withstand the long work hours, often working over sixty hours a week to meet the demands of the department. It is important to ask people where they have been and how often they are attending public functions such as a triage that is done when assessing patients to check into the hospital. Have your own personal triage to screen people, functions you plan to attend, and visitors in your home, whether family or not. There are a lot of people, especially young adults, who are COVID-positive yet asymptomatic.

This is why overlooking things can be dangerous. Some things that can carry COVID contamination are doorknobs, phones, and kitchen and bathroom cabinets. A good habit is wiping down all work areas with a disinfectant before using. Masks, though important, are not always good protection from COVID; they needed to meet medical-grade criteria since there are a lot of homemade masks. Face masks needed to be washed daily because coughing and sneezing in them also breeds contamination, which defeats the purpose. One rule I maintained was always keeping disposable masks on hand and keeping them in a Ziploc or container to prevent contamination from the environmental elements. Here is an idea of what a COVID lung looks like versus a healthy lung.

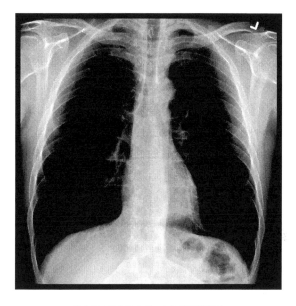

NORMAL CHEST

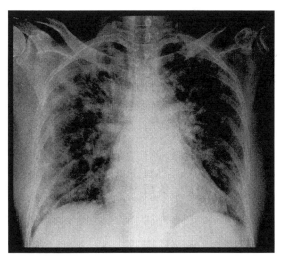

COVID CHEST

CHAPTER TWENTY:

VISION 2020—WHAT DO YOU SEE?

MYA SMITH-EDMONDS

Have you ever prepared plans in advance and remained hopeful that everything was going to turn out great?

Well, that was the game plan for many people all over the world in 2020. But, as the saying goes, "Life is full of surprises!"

As a McDonald's franchise owner of seven restaurants; each October, I do my business plan and projections for the following year. I planned to have a record-breaking year for 2020. The term "20/20" represents vision. So, I had a vision for a productive, efficient, and prosperous year. The year took off with a record-breaking start with high momentum, increased sales, increased guest counts, along with having great weather (at an otherwise usually snowy time). This was a winning combination. I am also a co-founder, with my dad, Harry L. Smith, Jr., of our foundation.

The Smith Foundation, Inc., is a 501(c)(3) non-profit organization established to reach, uplift, support, enhance the lives of, and empower all people to reach their full potential. Our purpose is to organize and maximize the power of simply "people helping people" to support communities in need and create a platform for people to experience the joy of serving. Our website is smithfoundationinc.com; you can log on to see videos and testimonies of the families, students, and children who have been blessed by the foundation and our generous sponsors and supporters! The cause receives 100 percent of the proceeds.

We have events that take place throughout the year to benefit multiple causes and areas of need such as college scholarships, Christmas toys, school supplies, food drives, coat drives, and more. We have given over $108,000 in scholarships, in the last two years ($4,000 each for twenty-seven students). We have provided toys, school supplies, food, and clothes for hundreds in need. There is such a huge need, now more than ever. The Smith Foundation, Inc., strives to produce top-rated events to benefit those in need. To reach more disadvantaged communities all over the world, we welcome sponsorships, help, and support of any kind because we know that we cannot do it alone. Again! The cause receives 100 percent of the proceeds.

We plan out our "Year of Giving" in November for the following year. We make our connections with the foundation supporters, volunteers, mentors, community groups, schools, students, food banks, sponsors, and so on. We plan out our events for the year because there are so many communities in need, and we really want to give ourselves the opportunity to support as many people as we possibly can. While flying high on optimism and momentum in my business and with the Smith Foundation, Inc., we approached the last month of the first quarter where we hit a brick wall: COVID-19, the pandemic.

COVID-19 came like a ghost in the night. We woke up one day, and the news kept reporting sickness and death at rapidly growing numbers day after day after day. People were becoming sick or dying from surface contact, airborne mucus, with 1.7 million deaths and still counting.

This was unheard of. My heart dropped as I continued to hear stories of our close ones getting sick or dying. This was devastating for us because although there was a pandemic and we had to practice social distancing, we knew that there were so many still in need. At this time with the foundation, we were not able to have events to raise funds to help the communities. This was so hard for us.

As soon as the States began to remove some of the stay-at-home orders, our foundation started doing community food drives, coats, hats, scarves, and gloves drives, Christmas toy drives, supplying masks and gloves to the community, and giving financial support to college students for tuition and other expenses, and more. We were just trying to find ways to help wherever we could without violating any state mandates. The recipients have been so grateful in this time of crisis. The food boxes are needed by so many because our unemployment rates reached a high of 14.7%, and more children are at home. The food boxes consist of various meats (e.g., chicken, turkey, ham, fish, wieners, sausage), produce, and dairy products. The students are so grateful because they are still on a mission to graduate (even if they have to take all classes online). They still have tuition to pay for. Christmas toys and gifts are the difference maker for so many children and families who do not have the means at this time. While everything else had been canceled all year, we could not cancel Christmas for our children who have been looking forward to a day of fun, celebration, and enjoyment.

It really made me see how important and impactful the children holidays (e.g., Easter, Halloween, Christmas) are. We had close to a hundred kids knock on our door for Halloween. They were fully dressed in their costumes in the spirit of fun from toddlers to teenagers. My face just lit up as I saw child after child come to the door. That is when I knew for sure our children needed the excitement of the fun holidays to get the opportunity to escape the reality and solitude of the despair that COVID-19 has brought into our world.

As a business owner when this crisis hit, I felt so much uncertainty about the future success of my business even though we were considered an essential business. The trends were changing for our customers, suppliers, vendors, and partners. The biggest devastation was for my employees because their family members were losing jobs, they had lowered household incomes, childcare was difficult, and they were concerned about their overall safety.

Many daycares closed, making it hard for employees to obtain childcare to come to work. I helped take care of my employees by helping to pay various bills for them (e.g., utility bills, car notes, medical bills, transportation, groceries) because I wanted them to know that I am here for them and that they are not alone in this struggle.

As my employees are essential workers, I rented a billboard that recognized all of my employees from various locations, gave them bonuses, gift cards, appreciation certificates, thank-you letters, appreciation celebrations, and so much more just to make sure they could feel my love and appreciation of them. I made sure my restaurants were continuously cleaned and sanitized throughout the day, and deep cleaned every night. I got protective shields, contactless payment, and so on to protect everyone. We did health checks each day on each employee. I did these things early, for the safety of my employees and guests. I wanted my employees to be able to be at work and feel a sense of safety, peace, joy, love, happiness, family, and appreciation. I appreciate them, their dedication, and their loyalty. I wanted the community to come in and feel safe, knowing that we were taking the extra precautions to protect them.

During this time, we provided free "Thank-You Meals" to all first responders in an effort to show our appreciation and gratitude for their work, sacrifice, and commitment. Even during this crisis, the team's hard work and focus achieved an increase in sales and cash flow and broke records in DT, digital, and delivery. As you can see, the pandemic brought a level of strain and uncertainty to our business and our foundation, yet we pressed forward to do all we could to give with the Smith Foundation, Inc., and to get results in business.

COVID affected my family in 2020. While I had some relatives test positive for COVID, they had a full recovery. I give all praise and honor to God for that! Also, this year was a huge milestone for my family with my dad's sixty-fifth birthday, October 4th. We did not get the opportunity to celebrate my dad as I wanted to because of COVID-19. But I decided to honor him with a "Letter of L.O.V.E." (Lifetime Legacy of Value Expressed). It reads:

Dad, when most people think of the number sixty-five, they think of retirement. Well, for anyone who knows you, they know that Harry L. Smith, Jr., and retirement could not possibly exist in the same sentence. You see operating in excellence and purpose as a way of life, making the most of every single day while being triumphant, inspirational, wise, faith-filled, loving, strong, caring, thoughtful, bold, humble, innovative, humorous, patient, encouraging, kind, respectful, determined, and hopeful! When I think of the number 10, symbolizing the tenth month in the year, October, I think of the number 10 in love. Love is divine and sacred. The meaning of 10 reveals that you are loved immensely. There is so much love for you among the people who treasure and value you.

When I think of the number 4, symbolizing the fourth day in October, I think of four distinct areas of significance that you have excelled in admirably: family and friends, business, giving back, and recognition (being honored). A good dad is one whose humor, personality, warmth, and wisdom have earned him the respect of his family and friends. Someone who makes this world a better place in which to live. You are an extraordinary dad.

One of the best things in life is having someone to laugh with and talk to while sharing the big and little moments of everyday. You are the kind of dad who makes a positive difference in our family and in the world. You bring love, hope, and inspiration. In your relationships with family and friends, you've always modeled 1Corinthians 13:4 and Ephesians 4:2-3 by expressing in your actions that love is patient, love is kind, by being patient, gentle, humble, and showing love, care, and respect.

You've always been an example and practitioner of wisdom in which your life is a reflection of Proverbs 3:16-17, "Wisdom gives a long, good life with honor, joy, riches, pleasure, and peace." Although the road has not been easy for you at all, you carved path and made a life for yourself and your family and have helped so many. Your strength and character show through your actions each and every single day.

Your resilience in life is a reflection of Romans 5:3-4, "Suffering brings perseverance, perseverance, character, and character, hope," as you have brought blessings and hope to your family, friends and the world, in so many ways. You have continued to passionately, press on in walking in your purpose from being a legend and a trailblazer across the US in McDonald's; being a real estate mogul in developing properties and building custom homes with your own Hearthstone Homes, giving of your time, gifts and treasures to so many in need as the philanthropic humanitarian that you are with the Smith Foundation, Inc., paying for college for your children to obtain a college degree and have an educational achievement, being debt free, and continuing to give beyond that; to even being recognized by the US House of Representatives with a Presidential Lifetime Achievement Award from Congresswoman Sheila Jackson Lee; being recognized by the Texas House of Representatives with a Community Service Award from State Representative Ron Reynolds: Humanitarian Award and honored in such a way that who you are and what you represent necessitates that October 4th be declared as the official "Harry Leonard Smith, Jr., Day" by Mayor of the City of Houston Sylvester Turner. You have given so much and been there with love and encouragement while living out your faith in practical ways. Dad, you ask for so little, but we owe you so much; you have carried your family on your shoulders, and always in your heart.

Looking at you, Dad, it's so easy to see, how phenomenal and what a stellar role model you've been for me.

You've taught me to think for myself from the start, to trust in my instincts, and follow what's in my heart. Your love, wisdom, teaching, character, and example have inspired me to stand tall and strong, and I will build on the legacy you've passed along. So, my hope for the future, whatever I do, is to be the example, I've seen in you! May your special day be just the beginning to many more decades of blessings, joy, opportunities, and favor and fulfillment in life. You are the best dad there could ever be! Happy Birthday Daddy!♥ I L♥VE YOU!!

This pandemic was such a trying time for so many of us. But I do believe that this was a season of opportunity. While I saw hardship, sickness, death, and misfortune, I also saw financial growth and opportunity that was given to some businesses and citizens; that could have been a stepping stone for innovation, creativity, new ideas, and new vision. It is all in how one "viewed" this year of vision. Hopefully, it made everyone see life through a new lens of hope and also to have a sense a preparation for the inevitable possibility of change. Now that 2020 is behind us, and we move into 2021

Five (2+0+2+1=5) represents favor and grace. Let's look forward and be in expectation of God's favor and grace for 2021. Let 2021 be the year that you throw your full self into what you believe you were created to do. You are known for "how" you serve! You serve so hard that others have to take notice. Be your best you! Show up in 2021. Remember Jeremiah 29:11, "'For I know the plans I have for you,' declares the Lord, 'plans to prosper you and not to harm you, plans to give you hope and a future.'"

CHAPTER TWENTY-ONE:
TESTING THE DEPTH OF STACEY LYNN

STACEY EMERSON

As if entrepreneurship isn't hard enough, 2020 hit us with a global shutdown no one could have imagined. It left most, if not all, types of careers and industries questioning whether they still will be around at the end of this. I remember the statewide shutdown on March 16th when I was told not to see any more kids for physical therapy. It was nerve wracking, to say the least.

I have never been one to stay in the house, let alone not work. (Inserts a scared yet irritated face.) At this point, my attitude was "this thing [COVID-19] is no big deal." It rarely affects the populations of people I work with, so why do I have to abide by this rule? Is this a government trick? The conspiracy theories and the questions were endless.

A few days passed, and I started to panic (internally). How am I going to pay my bills? What am I going to do? My business does not make enough for this massive shutdown. Thoughts of destruction began to fill my head. I found myself thinking (I know you do this too.) things like, "People won't want to buy clothes because we are at home, and they don't have anywhere to go."

By this time, a full bout of depression was trying to creep in, but being the woman of faith that I am, those thoughts only lingered until I realized all I needed was a strategic plan for ways to expand my online presence. Since everyone was at home, I knew that I could capitalize on it and allow my brand to be seen.

OK. OK. Let me be honest it may not have been that quick. I spent at least five days straight binge watching Netflix until I felt like I was a character in the show, *All American*. Man, how I loved Spencer and his drive. OK, back to reality. Before this I did not even know how to turn on my TV let alone get to Netflix. (P.S. Don't judge me. I spend most of my time working in one of my businesses.)

Yes, that is right. I have two businesses. I am owner of HER Treasures Boutique and lead wardrobe stylist of Stacey Lynn Style Studio. Now, maybe you can understand my initial panic. I am a fashion entrepreneur; work and sales were already far between, so for sustainability and consistency I used my license as a physical therapist assistant for children up to three years old as an independent contractor, which gave me flexibility and freedom to make my own schedule. Breaking into the fashion world was already hard; now I had to try doing it broke. It's really not an easy task, but now throw in government lockdown and everyone staying at home (cue the eye roll). To my great surprise, COVID would bring record-breaking numbers to my online store because, much like me, other people needed retail therapy, and online was the only place to get it. But the question is, "How did it happen?" Well simple, it was a conversation I had to have with myself and God. It went a little something like this.

I can remember praying and asking God what this whole thing meant and what He was trying to tell the world. To be honest, I cannot remember exactly what He said, and I am certainly not about to lie on God. I can, however, remember the actions that I began to take. Let me try to talk you through my thoughts. I was reminded of the plagues and calamity that the Bible speaks of and remembering that we should not be surprised but in all things pray without ceasing being aware that God sees all, and He knows all. COVID-19 was a surprise to us, but it did not hit God by surprise because he knew it and allowed it to happen.

I know you are probably reading this thinking, "What kind of God would allow something like this?" Well, I am glad you asked. It is the God of Abraham, Isaac, and Jacob, our savior Jesus Christ, that's who. He makes the sun rise on the evil and the good and rain on the just and unjust, meaning everyone. He sends judgment as well as grace and mercy. Usually, we do not experience the full wrath of God, and gratefully we are able to see His grace in events of disobedience, which is certainly only because He loves us more than we can imagine. But even in times of judgment, it is still God's way of correcting us which in turn is still loving us. So, don't get me wrong; many people have been affected adversely by COVID-19. They have lost loved ones and much more. But even in the midst of it all, it seemed like a chance for tables to turn and doors to open. We were all in the same place, no matter how rich, how famous, or how important we might be.

It was a chance for everyone to realize that they are just as human as the next person and no amount of money will protect them. So, even small businesses like HER Treasures Boutique and Stacey Lynn Style Studio could get their big turnaround by using the resource that we so commonly take for granted, social media. It became the way of life for everyone. All day, you can be in virtual parties, virtual shopping, and virtual dates. Yes, it was a time we never thought the world would come to see, but there we were. In that moment more than ever, I realized that every person left on earth still had a chance to get it right and a chance for their purpose to be fulfilled. That includes you!

This is when I made up my mind that I would not stop pursuing my purpose during this time but go harder and apply more pressure. So much in my spiritual life had changed right before the pandemic: February 1, to be exact. I was walking in a new level of understanding of the fullness of God's word that allowed me to really connect with God on a deeper level and understand my active duties as a Christian. As my eyes were opened to the Holy Bible by no longer being convinced of the traditions that were given to me but truly being transformed by the word that I had been reading for most of my life. I stopped looking at the Bible as stories and took it as factual events that took place in real life now having scientific facts to prove it. I started to understand the power that I had as a Christian and how I had been operating with only half of the power God gives those who believe in Him. My outlook on the pandemic became one of hope and possibility and not detriment. I reflected on the children of Israel in the time when they were in slavery, but because of one man's obedience and faith to believe in deliverance, things began to change. I reflected on what took place in the wilderness, and at that moment, I realized I could either complain or remember; I could sink or swim. I chose to remember that what God called me to do in fashion had not and would not miss me, but this was an opportunity to hone it.

I remembered that even in the midst of turmoil He is still able to bring out His people and raise them up much like he did Joseph, Moses, and Esther. So instead of sinking, I swam.

I swam with new ideas, new strategies, new connections, and I experienced the best year of my life in sales in both businesses. So, I don't write this to boast but to say we should choose to remember what God has done and not think about what He hasn't, choose to swim even when it feels like the water is overtaking you, chose to make your story a sequel and not the epilogue because you had the faith to believe God can show up for you too. In 2020, He did it for me, and surely I believe that He can and will do it for you.

So, our shutdown may have been COVID-19, a global pandemic, but yours can be debt, unbelief, or fear, but after reading this, I pray that you choose to believe the God of Abraham, Isaac, and Jacob and our Lord and Savior Jesus Christ is able to do exceeding and abundantly above all that we can ask or think not because of anything we have done but because of who He is. Choose to remember that there is no one above Him and that there is life outside of our jobs and everyday activities that require our attention. Our spiritual relationship with the ultimate creator, Jesus Christ, when everything else is shutdown, is still there as He labors on your behalf. It may be a journey, but it is a journey worth exploring.

CHAPTER TWENTY-TWO:

THE SUNSHINE IN THE DARK

SUNITA WHITE

My name is Sunita White, better known as Coach Sunshine! And I am a survivor of COVID-19.

Wow that was a mouthful, to say the least; 2019 was a prosperous and blessed year for my family. How many of you can relate? I hope more than one. Who would have thought after celebrating New Year's Eve to bring in a new year, life would change so drastically three short months later? Around the world people of all different walks of life and cultures would hear about something called COVID-19 or Coronavirus on the news. It began to spread across ABC, FOX, CBS, NBC, CNN, CNBC, and so many more news platforms. Then you began to read about the virus via blogs and magazines. Eventually what sounded like a China problem turned out to be a deadly global virus.

At the beginning of March of 2020 the cases of COVID-19 were 741,000, and the deaths stood at 13,175. By December 2020, more than 64.2 million cases were recorded worldwide. Out of those cases, 41.3 million cases recovered, and 1.49 million resulted in deaths. All of these numbers can be referenced from Google by simply typing in "COVID cases as of March 2020" and so forth. The source that Google referenced was the *New York Times*. Yes, take a moment and pause to breath because the numbers are certainly real and heartbreaking. When you watch people die on the television is one thing, but when it happens in your own backyard with people you love and know, it is tremendously catastrophic.

I had a lot of deaths occur around me because of COVID-19, and a few deaths that were not. I was not allowed to attend funeral services because the governor ordered no more than fifty people when having large gatherings. This prevented so many family and friends around the world from seeing their loved ones for a last time. Can you imagine how emotionally mortifying that is? Let's get deeper. Can you imagine having a Zoom call to view your loved one's funeral? I mean, times really changed in 2020 extremely fast.

Did I mention that as of May 1, 2020, masks were to be worn all the time in the state of Illinois? This was mandated by Governor JB Pritzker when the extension on the stay-at-home order was extended. If you were over the age of two, the US Centers for Disease Control and Prevention recommended everyone wear a cloth face covering in public and where social distancing was permissible (see https://www.illinoispolicy. org/what-illinoisans-need-to-know-about-the-may-1-mask-mandate).

For my family this was a problem since I have asthma and so does one of my children. I began to think how this would affect so many people around the world. I took the route to educate myself further instead of complaining about it. I went to https://community.aafa.org/blog/what-people-with-asthma-need-to-know-about-face-masks-and-coverings-during-the-covid-19-pandemic. This allowed me to learn how to make face masks with a sewing machine. More important, I saw how to wear the face masks properly for people with asthma. I will be transparent in saying that even after trying these methods, I would still have difficulty breathing after wearing the face mask for extended periods of time. So, ensuring that I timed how long I was in one store location made all the difference. When I felt anxious or would even have panic attacks, I would cut my trips short and stop shopping or whatever I was doing altogether and leave.

All right, summer is over. At this point for us parents with children, this means every child around the world should be preparing to be back in school. "Hooray" is what adults were thinking, I am quite sure, until reality settled in. Most schools start around August. Well, thanks to COVID, many school districts were affected, of course, and this caused start dates to be pushed back.

School began in September with an option to stay home or be hybrid. Staying at home meant online learning for five days. Hybrid meant going to school physically for two days and being at home for the other three days online, which quickly changed into all the children having to stay at home. So, the children never got a change to even be hybrid since COVID is so deadly.

Now, let's be clear, this is for Illinois school children. I know it was quite different in other states. Hey, but you catch my vibes. Like other parents, I began to think about what online learning meant for my family. I am a businesswoman. I have meetings, Zoom calls, phone conferences, traveling, emails, inventory, shipments, and so much more to keep up with. How am I going to continue being a businesswoman without being a bad parent?

With so many people being laid off around the world, my small businesses would have fewer clients/customers to place orders. Of course, I understood what was happening around the world, but this was literally my "ah ha" moment. I began to reflect on how I created Lit Dolls Boutique two years ago. Yes, some people will think that's still pretty fresh. This boutique helped me and so many people around the world. Even though there was a pandemic happening. I found out people still wanted to shop, look, and feel good.

That's what Lit Dolls Boutique is all about. You can find some more information at litdollsboutique.com. I am very fond of social media since everyone is using them nowadays. Please follow and share us with your family and friends. We may be found on Instagram and Facebook as "Lit Dolls Boutique." If you have any more questions, please email assistance@ litdollsboutique.com

Next, I zoomed in on my credit repair business, Sunshine Credit Repair, LLC. How many of you actually started to think about your credit once the pandemic was in full effect? Unfortunately, I am unable to see the number of hands being raised or the eyebrows. Sunshine Credit Repair, LLC will be there for you during a pandemic and even when the pandemic leaves. No matter who we are or what we do in life, we need good credit and should want excellent credit. People who had good and excellent credit were able to live on credit cards during the pandemic because they chose to get their credit in order. Good credit can be a life saver when you have a real-life crisis just like the COVID-19 tragedy. Do not let anything stop you from achieving your goals. Contact us today to schedule a free fifteen-minute consultation. I guarantee it will change your life.

We are on Instagram as and Facebook at "Sunshine Credit Repair LLC." You can fix your life at https://sunshine-credit-repair-llc.square.site. My team is waiting to assist you to get on the right track. Please feel free to email us at sunshinecreditrepair2@gmail.com

Last but not least, I spent my COVID restoration days paying special attention to my coaching business, Coach Sunshine, LLC. Do you remember I told you I'm better known as Coach Sunshine at the beginning of this awesome read? Well, I must admit coaching is my first love. The pandemic was a great time hone in on helping those in need. As I watched people fall into depression, some became suicidal, many lost jobs, and their income decreased, which caused financial struggles, reductions in health care, making decisions on how to put food on the table, and evictions, to name a few problems. I knew that I needed to keep my clients sane and secure. The ultimate goal was to keep everyone on track during such a traumatic time.

I want to extend this help to your family/friends. If you find yourself needing assistance with financial stability, business, coaching, staying goal oriented, mentally healthy, motivated with passion join my "Power Moves" membership platform. You can also check out my website coachsunshinellc.com. Don't hesitate to contact Coach Sunshine at motivation@coachsunshinellc.com. Sharing is caring. I am extending myself; be kind enough to share with a friend or family member who could use some Sunshine at this time.

CHAPTER TWENTY-THREE:

WHAT'S IN YOUR 'FRIDGE?
(A CRY FOR HELP)

SHARON BETTS

Heading toward the end of 2019, I started to reflect on what had happen during the year. The Lord had been speaking to me on a few things in my life. He had given me some instructions that were very specific, such as "increase your capacity in me," "remove limitations," and "remember the four Ps (plan, pray, prepare, prioritize)."

I cannot comprehend things as quickly as others because I got hit in my head a few years ago, and that has hindered me in my thought process. But, God! You see everyday things that people take for granted I struggle with, such as just getting out of bed, keeping focus whether listening, speaking, watching the television, or reading, which has always been difficult for me. So, my whole existence and my ability to function day-to-day was all God. Don't get me wrong. Where I am today is all credit to our Father, but I knew I needed more from God, or God needed more from me.

Was I ready to be honest before my Father?

I looked at the life of David. I remembered I had received a prophetic word stating that I was going to do great things, flow with word of knowledge, encouragement, and all the Godly things you can think of, and nothing is wrong with that, but for me that wasn't enough. Something was missing. Like a child, my relationship with my Father is important to me. I often tell my friends "I don't have a people problem, I have a God problem."

Our relationship with God is the oil that keeps our vehicle going, our financial oil, marital oil, and friendship oil for us to have healthy relationships we need to be right with God, and that starts with being honest with ourselves.

Time was running out, and I was running on empty. I was at rock bottom. My business was failing, marriage was failing, health was failing; my daddy was being placed in a nursing home because no one had the time to look after him, or should I say, cared enough to. I knew when I received the call that my poor daddy is going to be place in a nursing home, I knew I wouldn't see my daddy again. My heart broke because there was nothing I could do physically to help. I kept crying, "What more, God? What more? I am tired of everything."

Christmas came and went; everything was a blur. The only thing I wanted was to be still and quiet with the only person who can quench this ache and thirsting in my soul/heart. Every night I would pray, "God, I need a one-month break just to be alone with You," but I couldn't afford to be off work for that long being self-employed, so I dismissed the thought.

In March 2020 while at work, one of my clients said we were going on lockdown. I only responded to be polite, which just goes to show you where my head was at that time. She kept repeating that the whole country is going on lockdown. Then it finally sank in. What? I couldn't believe that God loved me enough to lock the whole county down. (Sorry guys; remember this is my story.). So, I could be with Him. How amazing!

Our God is such a loving Father, and He hears the cry of His children when we cry out in truth. I needed to reset, recalibrate, and basically get a spiritual detox. I needed to hear my Father's voice again. Then the news came no child wanted to hear, "Your dad has passed." I was numb to the touch. I didn't want to cry because if I did, I would not stop! The only thing I could say was, "God, I need You; God, I need you! In the mist of chaos, I need you!"

I could hear the Holy Spirit saying, but "What's in your 'fridge?"

I was like, "God, was I hearing clearly?" Like a child, I told my father, "I went shopping a few days ago, so I have lots in the 'fridge. Is someone coming to the house that I should cook dinner for?" As you know, our soul gets in the way of what God wants to do; we start reasoning things out. I am sure I am not alone.

Remember, I said I wanted more from God because He required more from us. Be careful what you pray for. Have you ever wanted something so badly, and when it finally happened, you don't know what to do with your time? That was me. Now COVID happened, and like many others, my question was, "What am I going to do?" I was exhausted. Again, I could hear the Holy Spirit saying, "What you don't confront, you cannot conquer."

Like a child in obedience, I went to my 'fridge, opened the door, and stared for about five minutes. Suddenly, the 'fridge took on a whole new look. I could hear my father saying, "I have been waiting for you. There is so much I want to reveal to you but you have a lot of things in the way. Your 'fridge is too full of unnecessary things."

I started crying because it was so true! If we look in the scripture, there are so many examples. Remember the story of the old wineskin in Matthew 9:14-17, Mark 2:18-22, and Luke 5:33-39? God is always looking for willing participants to partner with. He wants to expand Himself in us to make Himself larger.

For some, 2020 is the worst year, but for me it's my best year ever. I had allowed the Holy Spirit to remove the things I was carrying in my 'fridge (i.e., my life). Of course, my 'fridge maybe different from yours. I was so full of things, so much stuff and the hidden things trapped me in. The things we don't talk about because no one has time to listen to us. I had no vision for my life, business, or relationship. Everything was blurry. I couldn't see beyond February, 202. Nothing was flowing; I was so empty.

I knew deep down there was more in me.

I needed to yield myself totally to Him. I wanted God to remove everything that was in my 'fridge, but was I willing to let Him. We hold on to so many things like, past pain, and depending on where you are in your relationship with your savior, some of us hide behind things. God wants the true church (which is me and you) to be honest and say, "I am a mess," and "I need help." As far as I am concerned, I am the true church, and I was unhappy with me. The question still remains, "Am I willing?" Are you willing and obedient to allow God to change your agenda?

Immediately, I started pondering, and the very words Mary spoke (Luke 1:38) came out of my mouth, "Be it unto me according to your will." As soon as I surrendered my will, I could see the state of my 'fridge. God found me in the midst of chaos. He heard my cry. He chose me. All God wanted was a submissive attitude to His will. Little did I know my life was about to be changed.

About a month into lockdown, I received a call from an old friend; we began talking, and the rest is history. Everything about my life changed in an instant. Yes, you heard me right, in the blink of an eye. For the first time in my life, I could see clearly, I could see myself as how God sees me. I can see potential and purpose. God began unlocking gifts inside of me that I never knew existed. I wasn't afraid anymore. As I said, yes, God was able to move on my behalf. Life took on a new meaning. After coming out of lockdown July 10, 2020, clients started noticing. They would say, "You seem different." Different I was. I was seeing clearly. My business was now doing well, and my relationships were going great. I felt like a millionaire, literally.

During this time, I was able to:

- Reinvent my business

- Write my first book, *Umojah Afformation* (It's not just hair; it's your heart)

- Launch my exercise YouTube channel (Umojah Community Reggaesize)

- Create braiding courses

- Launch my audio version of (poetry in motion) will be available on CD

- Be a collaborative author with this book

- Work on my third book

God wanted me to live my best life in Him...

CHAPTER TWENTY-FOUR:

SURVIVING THE MOST FRIGHTENING 2020 MOMENT

ROSETTA HUTCHINSON

The year 2020 is one for the history books: no one was expecting this deadly virus called COVID-19 to sweep across the world like wildfire. It was so unexpected people everywhere panicked. Leaders across the world did not know what to do; even the doctors and nurses got confused with what to tell the nation. It reached the point where people began speculating, and world leaders began to blame each other for this deadly virus that has claimed the life of almost two million people globally; this was like a horror movie just happening before our eyes. COVID-19 seemed unstoppable; the world began to shut down left, right, and center. It was no respecter of anyone, the rich and the poor and middle class were clueless even in the country where I and my family reside; it was like a ghost town.

There was a sudden economical halt, businesses were affected, a lot of people lost their jobs, children could not go to school, and churches and restaurants were closed. There was nowhere to meet and greet; family and friends had to stay their distance, so many people panicked because of this deadly virus that no one can see. It was like an invisible man ripping people's bodies apart. Everyone was looking around trying to gather groceries at the supermarket. Even in the pharmacies, we could not get vitamins of any kind just to fight this deadly virus or products to keep our homes clean. Mask and gloves, sanitizers, and other household items went scare. Some stores even inflated their price on essential goods like toilet paper.

You see, when COVID-19 was happening in China, it was nobody else's business until it started to affect one of the most powerful countries where people were dropping like flies. It was so unbelievable; hospitals began to get overcrowded; they even started to run out of ventilators. The morgues were packed to capacity until they had to get make-shift morgues.

Oh, my God, it was so sad. People were losing their loved ones, especially in the nursing and retirement homes.

Turning on my TV to watch CNN, CP24, and ABC watching the numbers of death rise, friends and families getting sick, and everyone just being confused really hurt. Being a personal support worker working with the elderly, I had to use caution because the virus was in the nursing home like crazy. It was as if life had no meaning. I saw people just dying through no fault of theirs or ours, but because most of these people had underlying illnesses. The virus attacked their bodies. I was so scared some days, I did not want to go to work, but because of what I signed up for, I could not just pull myself out. But my life was at risk as well. I had a family to go home to, and while I prayed for God's mercy, I really could not stand the sight of what was happening. Being a frontline worker, I have learned so much, especially to have empathy toward the elderly. In times like this, we have been their family because they were not allowed to have any visitation by anyone from the outside. It was so lonely for some of them knowing that they used to see their family daily. I cried for them and also for myself, asking God when this would end. My heart goes out to all who lost their loved ones that season. I kept saying, "This too shall pass."

I remember a vision I had, and in it God said, "You are looking to the people that I made for direction, seek Me, and you will get the answers about what is happening around you."

The fear that I had about this virus was my worst nightmare. I had to get tested because of the job. I was hoping and praying I did not catch the virus. One day, I began to feel a bit off in my body, but I did not really pay much attention to it, then my head got tender, my tongue lost taste, and my eyes began to hurt, but still I ignored the signs. Soon after, my supervisor told me to get tested. I still waited a week until after Mother's Day. I joined the long lines waiting for hours seeing people of all races, sizes, and shapes, but when you looked in their faces you could see that they were scared as I was.

Everyone in their masks looked as if we were going to the gas chamber, but I kept on praying to God "Please don't let it be what I am thinking; please don't take me from my children. I have not seen them grown past the worst yet. I need to live to see my grandkids, and most off all, I haven't even begun to do the work You called me to do." I was really crying in my heart. I said to God, "Please forgive me for my sins knowing and unknowing." I felt devastated, and little did I know that I had already caught it.

I was in the kitchen cooking when my phone rang. I answered it. On the end of the line a lady asked if this was Rosetta Hutchinson. I said yes.

Then she said, "I am calling from the Health Department," and at that moment my heart stopped, and I was numb. I asked her to hold on so I could put my phone on speaker for my sons to hear the devastating news. Then she said, "You have the virus, and you need to quarantine for fourteen days."

My God, I cried. That day was the worst day of my life because it was like a death sentence. Anyway, I finished preparing dinner for my two boys, Gabriel and Daniel. Then I started to prepare my things to stay in my room for the fourteen days. I was really trying to enjoy the day with my boys, but I just could not. I made a few phone calls to my relatives at home in Jamaica, requesting prayers. I also called my relatives here in Canada; they all reached out to me to comfort me and give me assurance that it would be OK. Down inside I just felt empty and alone. I prayed, had a warm bath, and went into my room. I pulled back the covers from my bed, and went in to get some rest, but as night fell it got worse. I began to have shortness of breath. Anxiety began to take over my body. I was so restless I stayed up the whole night fighting the fear of death. When I tried to lie down, I could feel like something was rushing from my feet up to my brain, and I would jump up off the bed. I was so scared.

Monday morning I got up and began to get worse. I felt like needles were sticking me all over my body. I could not contain myself. I told my son to call 911, as I prepared to go I began to tell my boys where everything was located. I told them I loved them so much, and then the paramedics arrived all geared up because they don't want to catch the virus from me.

They put me on the stretcher, checked my vitals, and were trying to talk to me to keep me awake.

I remember my son telling me "Mom, I will drive behind the ambulance," even though he would not be able to come in. The tears began to roll down my face as my heart began to beat faster than normal. My body did not feel like mine, as if I were in a different zone. While in the ambulance, I told one of the paramedics to keep on talking to me because that let me feel a bit better.

He replied to me, "Sure, whatever makes you feel comfortable."

On reaching the hospital, we went underground in a different area. I asked him why. He said to me because of the virus we have to be in an isolated area. When he opened the doors of the ambulance, I was scared. I asked him to hold my hand, which he did. All I wanted was God and comfort. Then he said to me that another person would come and get me and take me inside When I looked up, I saw this man in a full suit of white. He introduced himself, took me inside, and placed me in an isolated room all by myself. The room was all glass with a telephone on the wall, a wash basin, and no one else in sight. At that moment I began to have a reality check. As I was lying on the bed, I felt like my lungs were shutting off. My mind was all over the place. I realized I needed Jesus more than ever, but I kept on talking to God while I was in the room.

I saw my son's name on the wall, Daniel. His name gave me hope. I began to remember the story of Daniel in the lion's den and how Jesus delivered him by shutting the mouth of the lions so I knew He would shut away this virus from me. I stood up and began to worship like never before. I could feel the presence of God with me. As I ask Him why, He said to me, "For you to tell your story, I had to inflict you to go tell my people this is no joke, and it is just the tip of my finger. Write your story of all you experience, the pain you went through but I God is with you always."

By this time I heard a knocking on the door. I looked down; it was the nurse who came in with a machine to run some test on me; she did a heart test, blood work, x-rays, and a CAT scan. After a brief moment, she told me to listen for the phone on the wall to ring. The doctor would speak to me from there. I spent the entire day there, and then the doctor said my heart was beating too fast so they put me on a drip to calm me. What I realized was that no one wanted to come close to me, for which I could not blame them. Even when the nurse was putting in the drip, I could see how scared she was, but she just had to do her work.

After a couple of hours, I was done, and they released me and said if the breathing got worse I must come back, but I should go home and stay in isolation. Before going into isolation, I tried an old time Jamaican remedy with the onion, garlic, ginger, and turmeric with oranges, lemon, and a lot of boiled water just to get this virus out of my system. It was not easy at all; there were nights I could not sleep in my bed. I had to sit up in my chair and sleep because of the feeling that I had to lean on my side even if I wanted to lie down. Sometimes I had to lean my back against the wall and stretch my hands in the air just to release my lung to breathe in and out. Everything that I had to drink had to be hot, even the water I drank, because the virus cannot survive in a hot body. The remedies helped me to pass out the virus even when I peed or had a bowel movement. Although that was a good sign, the trick was people cannot sleep on their back with this virus because they could suffocate. That was how a lot of people died. I also steamed my face a lot, so the mucus in my head and lungs passed out.

It was a learning process for us all, Christian or not. While I was suffering with COVID-19, God even allowed me to pray for someone who had lost her fiancé. I never knew I had such strength even though I was recovering from the disease myself. My family and friends told me how strong I was, but sometimes I doubted myself. As I reflected on how Job in the scriptures went through his trauma, I started to believe how strong I was and how God was the ultimate cause of my strength. After three weeks, I had to return to my doctor to get tested to make sure the virus had left my body, but I had to wait three more days for the result, which came back negative.

I was so happy, but I took some more time off from my job just to build up my body. The good thing is, the government offered us a subsidy so I could take care of myself and Daniel and Gabriel, which I appreciate so much. Those two boys never left my side. They did everything in their power for me to get well and for my aunt. To God be the glory.

During all this I had to realize that so many family and friends looked up to me and appreciated me, especially my loving mom. This was really a time of reflection on life, who supports me, and who God is in the moments when nothing else really matters. When I was faced with death, all I wanted was for God to just spare me, and I would do anything for that. I had put off my God-given assignment for so long, only using God like He was an ATM machine. I was wrong. God is a jealous God, and He does not like it when we only call upon Him in the times of need and trouble.

These days, we all need God. We must seek His face and worship Him. I know He called me by name, and I know the generation to come will hear and read about this deadly virus that some people lived through while others did not, but to God be the glory that I did just to tell my story and my experience. I know my great, great, grandchildren will be able to read about their grandma Rosetta and how she survived something for the history books.

CHAPTER TWENTY-FIVE:
LET'S SUM THIS ALL UP!

DEI TATUM

Writing is the art and science, a life application, and a methodology of the expression of one's thoughts, actions, feelings, and phenotypes. Writing embodies various modes of discourse such as descriptive, expository, persuasive, narrative, technical, and poetic, all of which have the goal to speak and captivate the audience to maintain their attention and interest.

People unknowingly write every second, every minute, and every hour as they perambulate throughout their daily lives. When people sleep, they are unconsciously writing. When people wake, daydream, eat, drink, sing, or dance, they are writing and speaking through body language, through movement, and song. People's thoughts, actions, and responses to their environment speak. To reiterate, people are writing unknowingly. People's lives are scribed without their knowledge unless it is revealed and are edited by One Who is higher than you and I. No one knows another person's story, or their expression, or deepest secrets. No one can truly see a person's scars, life challenges, open and incurable wounds, or confessions. No one knows a person's unspeakable language even when it is written in any mode.

One thing certain is that twenty-six strangers who lived through one pandemic in one year were able to write their stories. Writing is intentional and should be purposeful. Writing is known to many as a response to people, places, and things around us or that involve us. Here, I will share my thoughts about 2020 and COVID-19 in poems of different genres for different audiences.

Expressions to My Children:

Various Poems

COVID-19 like Thunder

Acrostic Poem

Tremble, terrible, tumultuous, tasteless, tortuous sound.

Hover, haunted, harrowing, dark like a ghost that peregrinates around.

Under a tree, a rock, on roof-top, in a house, a car, for shelter,

Never mind, I will stand still, because the sun will decimate her.

Dancing, frowning, smiling across the eerie looking sky,

E ager to make people run, hide, weep, and put the world to silence. I don't know why?

Racing for freedom, peace, tranquility, sanity, and justice for all.
Hear the pounding sound of footsteps approaching to devour
and consume the aching souls of all.

COVID-19—Fierce

A Cinquain Poem

Dragon
Dangerous, Grim
Devour, Terrifying
Consuming, Fetid Breath, Fly, Leap
Wyvern

Figurative Language Poem.
Cherry Tree Represents Humanity and Gallantry during the COVID-19 Pandemic

In my grandmother's cherry orchard, lies a Cherry Tree.
Standing tall, picturesque, valiant, and dauntless,
Winking eyes, whistling, narrowed lips and waving at me.
Like snow on the ground,
Like rain falling from the sky drip! drop! drop!
Tilting over, tumbling leaves that will never stop!
Spreading wide as the Grand Canyon, long as the Nile River,
With tenacity and brevity, the limbs will make your heart
quiver.
The Cherry Tree is a tower, stands with tenacity and power,
Vigilant and keen, every second, minute and hour.
The cherry orchard as grandiose as the Seven Wonders of the
World and the seven seas,
Go on an odyssey to possess and conquer all! Just you and the
tree.

COVID-19 Stain
Haiku Poem with (Tercet)

Jobless, homeless, poor
Been through Depression since birth.
Hear the nation cry.

Law and Politics

Law Enforcement During the Corona Virus (COVID-19) Pandemic

Color Poem

Blue Hero

Blue stands in attention, ready to take on the duties of the day.

Blue says goodbye to its' family when it goes away.

Blue sees and tastes the terrors that lurk in the night.

Blue is ready to defend, take armor and fight.

Blue is the ocean that calms the confusion and the strife.

Blue is the wind that blows in every direction to save a life.

Blue is honest, a protector, a mentor, do you know what I am seeing?

Blue touches the soul and the depths of a troubled human being.

Blue has no color, is no color, do you understand what this mean?

Blue calms and smells the storm of every heart and makes it dance and sing.

Blue is love, patience, kindness, understanding and respect of mankind.

Blue will never leave a person in the worst condition behind.

Blue comforts every man, woman, and child on its shoulder.

Blue cannot wait until this pandemic is over.

Blue works overtime, day and night and no rest at all.

Blue continues with pride, integrity, respect and stands tall.

Blue says to the other colors, "Stand up, take cover and do what's right."

Blue says, "Don't let us just be the beacon of light."

Blue anticipates and hears other challenges that lie ahead in this world.

Blue is ready to combat for every young boy and little girl.

Blue remain you, in everything that you do,

Remain humble, no matter what changes, you always remain Blue.

Because you're my hero and you're '*bleutiful*' too.

Narrative Poem with (Rhyme Scheme)

911 Code Red, White and Blue

Hurry! Hurry! Hurry! Police sirens everywhere!

Chaos, noise, screams, fights, yelling, cursing… what a nightmare!

"Calm down, calm down; it's OK. Just breathe."

"I can't, I can't, gargle.. goggle… cough… cough! Please don't leave."

"Is there anyone home? Who's upstairs?" "My grand mom and her son."

"I need an ambulance here immediately. Oxygen…1...2...3."

This life we have won.

"Hooray! She did it!" Out she walks with a thankful face looking up at the sky.

She smiled and looked down at the child and wiped the tear from her eye.

"It's alright now she's going to be fine." and put a lollipop in the girl's hand.

She smiled through the mask, and said, "This pandemic I don't understand."

Go away! Do not come back! Just leave us all alone!

Do you have another planet to terrorize and roam?

Fear, anxiety, restricted and can't travel around to any places.

Anger, frustration, mourning, the unknown is all on their faces.

Social distancing is smart, but will it work for the people now?

Cases are increasing worldwide and you're going to ask how?

"911 what is your emergency?" "My mom is not breathing! Can you please come quick?"

The heartbeat stops, "Oh my God!" is what you hear. "I think I am going to be sick."

"911 Can I help you? Hello? 911, Hello? Are you there?"

A calm deep voice that sounds far away says, "Yes I am. I am EVERYWHERE."

"Hello? Excuse me?" The dispatcher got quiet and scratched his head.

Thinking about the tone and what that voice on the other end said.

"I answered the prayer of the little girl and the woman that went to the rescue.

I just saved your brother, your mother and your wife too."

"Thank you! Thank you! Thank you!" as he looked to heaven
and said, "I know this is YOU!"

"I just want to give a special Thanks to the Woman in Blue!"

So, the next time you see the police, medical personnel, EMTs
to name a few.

Just give a nice shout out to code red, white, and blue!

Rhymed Poem with (Assonance)

ROTUS (Revival of the United States)

Have you seen POTUS, FLOTUS OR SCOTUS?

and where is that DOTUS?

Abandoned the nations and left without notice.

You said you were for us,

But COVID has smote us,

You fire doctors and scientists,

And tell them to motus.

The plague of the locust,

Has been released upon us.

Fever and shallow breathing,

That's the prognosis.

Prayer and prevention should be our focus.

In case you didn't notice, all the rhetoric and lies you've told
us,

Thousands of bodies have suffered necrosis.

We pray for a Moses, a vaccination is told to us,

Gives us stimulus checks to keep us under your hypnosis,

I feel like I am Jonas, in the belly of the oceans.

I am a Poetess and my name is not Lois.

COVID is ferocious, people are dying with slowness,

Prideful, heartless speeches as you stand in remoteness.

Ignorance, hatred, and racism you've shown us. You believe
that you're above us. This is a democracy not a dictatorship,
and you think that you own us.

Now Joshua is for us, and he will drive us and direct us

To the promise land and nothing can stop us. So, America, let's
refocus. Worship and pray to God because he knows us. Let's
get back on the right track, because it is owed to us. God Bless
America.

Spiritual Poem with (Rhyme Scheme)

The Quintessence of the I AM in the mist of COVID-19

I AM the epitome of time, the genesis of humanity subsistence,

I AM the Alpha and Omega, the beginning of sublime and the
end of malevolence.

I AM Spirit and Truth, Love and Eternal Life,

I AM the husband and the bride - groom and I AM searching
for a

"Spot without wrinkle wife."

I AM omnipotent, omnipresent, omni-patient, and omniscient,

I AM omni-dimensional, omnifarious, omnibenevolent and efficient.

I AM GOD the Father, GOD the Son and GOD the Holy Spirit,

I AM the Ark of the Covenant so be careful how you approach and come near it.

Clean hands and a pure heart are things that I seek,

Not prestige, fame, vain-glory, or worldly gains...but the lowly and meek.

I AM Jehovah Shalom, Jireh, M'Quaddesh, Elohim, and Nissi.

I AM Jehovah T'sidkenu, Shammah, Saboth, Rohi and Rophe.

I AM El-olam, Berith, Gibbor, Roi, and Shaphat,

I AM El-Elyon, Shaddai, Elohim, Adonai and Palet.

I AM the Gate for the Sheep, The Governor, Nazarene, The Rock and High Priest,

I AM Master, Mediator, Lord of Lords, and the Prince of Peace.

I AM the Rock, The Rose of Sharon, Root of David, Ruler of GOD 's Creation,

I AM the Head of the Church, The Holy One of Israel, and the Horn of Salvation.

I AM the Good Shepherd, Gift of GOD, Friends of Sinners, and the Foundation,

I AM the Everlasting Father, Faithful and True Witness, and the Desire of All Nations.

I AM King of Kings, The Deliverer, Chief Cornerstone,

I AM Head of the Corner, Comforter and the Bishop of Souls I take home.

I AM the Perfector of Your Faith, The Anointed One, The Almighty and I can Bless,

I AM the Advocate, Lamb of GOD, Lion of Judah, Living Water, and the Tree of Righteousness.

I AM the door, the Road called Straight, the Diamond, The Eye, and the City Set on a Hill which cannot be hid.

I AM the Forgiver of All sins, regardless of what mankind did.

I AM the Restorer of the Breach, Repairer of the Broken Hearted, and those who live in poverty or dearth.

I AM the One that gave permission for the pandemic to pervasively roam this earth.

Just know that I subsist, and I am here, there… I am everywhere and just BE,

I AM the CHRIST, I AM that I AM, and I AM who they say I AM…. I…AM HE!